Purchasing Computers

PURCHASING COMPUTERS

A practical guide for
buyers of computers
and computing equipment

Edward R. Sambridge

amacom
A DIVISION OF AMERICAN MANAGEMENT ASSOCIATIONS

Library of Congress Cataloging in Publication Data

Sambridge, Edward R.
  Purchasing computers.

  1. Computers–Contracts and speciations–United States. 2. Computers–Purchasing. I. Title.
KF905.C6S25   1981   001.64'068'7   81-66234
ISBN 0-8144-5682-0   AACR2

© 1979 Edward R. Sambridge
First published by Gower Press, England.
Published in the U.S.A. in 1981 by AMACOM,
a division of American Management Associations, New York.
All rights reserved. Printed in the United States of America.

This publication may not be reproduced, stored in a retrieval system, or transmitted in whole or in part, in any form or by any means, electronic, mechanical, photocopying, recording, or otherwise, without the prior written permission of AMACOM, 135 West 50th Street, New York, N.Y. 10020.

First Printing

Foreword

For more than 20 years the computer industry, by which should be understood not merely the production and sale of computing equipment but also the total organization and economics of its use, has been one of the oddities of business life, since it is dominated by the sellers, not by the buyers. There are a number of reasons for this state of affairs, and a variety of ways in which it shows, but one of the clear signs that it is so lies in the extent to which the supply of equipment is legally governed by manufacturers' standard contracts.

These contracts vary from manufacturer to manufacturer, but they have one thing in common: any doubts and any marginal points are in favor of the seller. If it were not so, then human nature and self-preservation would have been turned upside down.

It is thus with the greatest pleasure that I welcome Ted Sambridge's attempt to establish model terms which, as far as I can judge, establish a degree of equity between buyer and seller in this marketplace. As they become used—and it is important that they are used and are known to have been accepted by manufacturers A, B, and C—they will eliminate a great deal of wasted time on both sides of this agreement before and after the supply of the equipment. In my judgment, it will put this most modern of industries where it should have been ten years ago.

GERRY FISHER
Former President
British Computer Society

Preface

Not so long ago, acquiring a computer was the start of an exciting venture into the largely unknown. The term "acquiring" is used rather than buying, because it was not always possible to buy a machine even if you wanted to; many machines were available only on rental terms. In those days software was in its infancy and although the number-crunching ability of the computer was obvious, the potential for data processing and control functions was only slowly beginning to be realized.

In those heady days the excitement was in exploring the data processing potential, and spectacular successes and equally spectacular failures were all part of the game. Mundane matters such as contractual assurances for performance were hardly considered, (After all, system performance was not the basis on which machines were supplied.) In any event, in rental contracts there was usually a termination clause which enabled the user, in theory at least, to return the machine without penalty after the specified period of notice.

So much has changed since those days!

National and international trading patterns and economic scenarios have altered drastically. Recurrent materials shortages, political interventions in markets, increased legislation, recessions, financial constraints, and high interest rates have resulted in battered gross margins and have forced companies to look far more closely at their investments than they did, say, 20 years ago.

The precocious computer industry has not only developed with the speed that one has come to expect from any new, high-technology industry; it has far outstripped most of our early expectations. The price-performance ratio in hardware has improved to an extent where even the smallest businesses can afford a computer. Indeed, the question might be asked, "Can they afford *not* to have one?" The speed of computer operation, the capacity of memories, and the developments in data transmission (facilitating distributed computing and on-line operations), together with a host of ingenious peripherals, have extended the computer's horizons into applications unsuspected in the early days.

These hardware developments have been made possible only by the parallel improvements in software, and indeed the current trend in the computer industry is to spend more and more time and money on the development of both operational and application software. If much of the hardware now available can be described as ingenious, then software must be praised even more.

In short, the last two decades have seen enormous changes both in the broad commercial scene and in computing technology; the only thing that has not changed has been the commercial attitude of the computer manufacturers. The computer manufacturers have continued to insist on the application of their own Conditions of Sale, despite the problems that this can cause the buyer. In the early days these problems were not acute, user skills as much as the manufacturers' skills developed applications, and it would have been unreasonable for a user to expect assurances on system performance. However, with the changes in commercial environment and computing technology, the attitude of the manufacturers can no longer be considered reasonable. Some examples will help illustrate my point.

With the more stringent economic circumstances that currently apply, few companies are prepared to sanction the acquisition of new and expensive equipment unless a satisfactory return on capital can be demonstrated. To this end, computer managers are now being required to justify *in economic terms* their demands for capital. This means that the projected usage must be expressed in a tightly written specification against which performance can be monitored. But what use is this if there is no legal understanding on performance, or even criteria for acceptance? Financial advisers are taking a greater role in defining the basis of cost-performance evaluations, cost-benefit analyses in relation to anticipated performance, and the date of the commencement of that performance. But what confidence can customers have in such analyses

Preface ix

when the computer manufacturers will not give guarantees of delivery?

The situation is even worse for the small businessman who knows virtually nothing about computer technology and is sold a system to perform a specific task. In the absence of written understandings from the supplier that the task will be performed for the money that the buyer has agreed to pay, where does he stand when the specified performance is not achieved with the equipment supplied?

The glib answer to these questions is usually that the buyer has legal recourse, but this is expensive and time-consuming and the outcome is uncertain, since it is dependent on the courts' interpretation of the intent of the parties at the time the contract was signed. But in practice, only a small percentage of users are prepared to gamble on starting a legal action against the manufacturers, many of which are multinational giants. The easiest, but most expensive, way out is to buy that extra black box that is sure to satisfy the users' requirements until it can be demonstrated that yet another black box is needed.

A computer salesman is reputed to have said that most data processing installations are sold, while only a minority are actually purchased. Yet computer purchasing is not the esoteric operation that many computer experts and most computer salesmen make it out to be, and, with practical guidance and advice, anyone with commercial experience should be able to place workable contracts for computer equipment in a way that ensures the protection of the organization.

It was with this in mind, and in recognition of the problems involved, that the Institute of Purchasing and Supply (IPS, the professional institute representing buyers throughout the United Kingdom, and one of the premier organizations of its kind in the world) asked me to form a working group to examine the problems.

When I began my study, it quickly became apparent that many buying organizations were aware of the problems and I was fortunate to be able to work with a group in which commercial, technical, and legal expertise were represented. Furthermore, the group had the tremendous advantage of being currently engaged in the "sharp end" of the business: the problems we were trying to solve were those that were currently being experienced by the group members. Detailed investigations showed that there was a wealth of technical literature on hand and a few very good books on general commercial/legal aspects. But there was available to buyers no comprehensive document that could be presented to manufacturers with their invitation to bid and that spelled out the terms under which they wanted to do business.

It was to provide such a purchasing tool to computer users that the working group produced a set of Model Conditions of Contract, which provide an equitable trading framework within which contracts that are fair to both parties can be drawn up.

The IPS work on Model Conditions of Contract in the United Kingdom evoked interest in many other countries, including the United States, Canada, Australia, Sweden, Norway, and the nations of the European Economic Community (EEC). Indeed, the interest in the EEC has now been formalized, and regular meetings of the Contractual Links Working Group of the Committee of European Computer Users' Association of which I am the Secretary, are being held. That group is working toward formulating Model Conditions of Contract that could be introduced throughout the EEC.

There is a widespread feeling that many manufacturers' Conditions of Sale should be replaced by something more equitable, and it is for individual customers to insist that their rights be reflected in the Conditions of Contract applicable to their purchases. The IPS Model Conditions of Contract and the explanations of the individual clauses contained in this book should provide computer users with the tools to achieve that end.

The IPS Working Group on Contract Conditions is currently considering further sets of Model Conditions for Maintenance, Rent/Lease, and Maintenance and Software. When these are published, they will further aid computer users in obtaining equitable terms.

During the deliberations on the Model Conditions of Contract, it was recognized that the main set of conditions is comprehensive enough to cover user requirements ranging from micro- and minicomputers and peripherals to mainframe equipment and comprehensive systems based on mainframes, but they are more complicated than those needed for the smaller items of stand-alone equipment when the purchase is fairly straightforward. For this reason the Shortened Form was produced, thus covering the requirements of users of large configurations down to the users of the smaller systems.

The core of this book is, therefore, Chapters 4 and 5, which give the rationale and explanation of the clauses in the OPS Model Conditions of Contract. These should be sufficient to enable a competent buyer to obtain satisfactory contract terms, although they do not give sufficient aid to the small and first-time users who do not regularly procure computer equipment. To fill that void, additional material has been introduced giving information and specimen documentation on how to invite bids and how to conclude a satisfactory contract. There is also a chapter specifically for the small and first-time user who needs to know how to approach computer usage from scratch. This takes the reader through the process of need assessment, justification, evaluation of alternatives, selection of the system, and installation and commissioning.

Finally, I would like to acknowledge the contributions of all those people who have been involved in the production of both the Model Conditions of Contract and this book. They are too numerous to mention individually, but that does not detract from my appreciation of their individual contributions.

But I must record my debt of gratitude to an American business associate and friend, Joanne M. Matteucci. Joanne has worked in the United States for a number of computer manufacturers, and is currently a resident of Britain, where she is working as an independent computer consultant and computer journalist. Joanne has edited the British version of this book to produce an American version, which not only reflects the slight changes in commercial practices between the countries, but also substitutes American usage for the British English in which this book was originally written.

EDWARD R. SAMBRIDGE

Contents

1	Model Conditions of Contract and Conditions of Sale	1
2	Contract Documentation	11
3	Small and First-Time Users	29
4	Model Form of Conditions of Contract for the Supply and Installation (Purchase) of Computer Equipment	37
5	Shortened Form of Model Form of Conditions of Contract for the Supply and Installation (Purchase) of Computer Equipment	119
	Postscript	137

Purchasing Computers

1

Model conditions of contract and conditions of sale

Conditions of Contract and Conditions of Sale can perform a useful administrative function in defining methods of dealing with contractual situations and other day-to-day details, but it is hoped that they need never be referred to in order to resolve disputes. It can be argued that, in relation to disputes, specific conditions relating to the transaction are not necessary, since one always has recourse to litigation. The problem is that contracts in the field of computing are becoming increasingly complex, and a clear definition of the requirements and obligations of the parties is necessary to avoid misunderstandings, particularly since large numbers of individuals are often involved. Recourse to litigation is a time-consuming and expensive business, and there is no guarantee that the outcome will confirm the intent of the parties; indeed, there may never have been a true consensus when the contract was first signed.

Conditions of Contract or Sale which are understood and accepted by both parties at the outset provide a number of clear advantages:

Definition. Communication, even in the simplest of situations, is difficult, and computer contracts are seldom simple. In most cases, individuals from different disciplines are involved, and this alone ensures that different interpretations can be applied to the same situation. For example, a computer manufacturer's technical representative may make the statement, "We shall be responsible for installation and setting to work." Technically he will do just that—but who pays? Is the price included in the cost of the equipment? Has the customer any rights of inspection and rejection? These and similar matters are defined in the contract, of which the conditions play an essential part.

Unforeseen circumstances. When two parties enter into a contract, they do so in the expectation that the customer will get what he wants, when he wants it, and at the agreed price. The manufacturer's expectation is that nothing will prevent him from achieving what the customer wants and that he will receive a profit from the transaction. Unfortunately this does not always happen; the customer's information to the manufacturer may be inaccurate, or the manufacturer may have underestimated the difficulties involved in meeting the customer's requirement and thus sees his profit margin being eroded. When difficulties arise, it is time-consuming and frustrating to establish the liabilities of each party without conditions that specifically define their respective rights and obligations.

Therefore, Conditions of Contract and Conditions of Sale should state who is responsible for what in terms of both technical performance and cost.

Discipline. Both manufacturers' and customers' managements should recognize the value of Conditions of Contract and Conditions of Sale as tools of management. The more complicated a project, the more chance there is of something going wrong and, perversely, the more chance of staff people assuming the attitude that if they keep their fingers crossed, it will all work out in the end.

It is common experience that difficulties do not just go away; complications occur and projects can rapidly degenerate into chaos when matters are left to chance. Although it would be difficult to establish, there appears to be a correlation between the difficulties encountered on a project (and the additional costs) and the degree of vagueness in the original contract documentation.

Commercial relations. How many times does one hear the question, "Why do I need to spend time on formal contracts? My supplier has to be on the up and up with me — my business is far too valuable to him." But what does this attitude really achieve, and who benefits?

If the customer is big enough and the manufacturer is heavily dependent on his business, then he will clearly wish to avoid antagonizing his customer and he will often be prepared to give way on small matters. However, he must make a profit to stay in business, and in the long run it is his customers who will pay. The large customer may benefit at the cost of the smaller customer in the short term, but even with the larger customer there is a limit to the extent to which the manufacturer can give way. If giving way means severe cash-flow problems or even bankruptcy, then he will fight. Whatever the circumstances, it will benefit the manufacturer to have his responsibilities clearly defined so that he can price his obligations. Contracting is, after all, a question of the allocation and pricing of resources and hence involves risk. There is little advantage to the manufacturer in increasing the risk element.

The more common situation is that the small customer is confronted with a set of the manufacturers' Conditions of Sale (which leaves many points unstated) and a take-it-or-leave-it attitude. What is the position of the small customer in such circumstances? If he enters into a contract on that basis, how much weight does he carry with a large, multinational computer manufacturer? The requirements of the small user are dealt with more thoroughly later in this book, but it is sufficient to point out here that equitable conditions of contract are highly desirable from everyone's point of view, particularly the small customer's.

MANUFACTURERS' CONDITIONS OF SALE

In the consideration of any matters relating to computers, it is difficult to avoid making reference to IBM, since its dominant position in the industry means that it sets most of the technical and commercial standards. It is unfortunate that IBM seems unable to forget that its computer commercial roots were in rental and leasing and that in extending its Rent and Lease Conditions to cover purchases, it has produced a relatively small set of conditions that protect IBM but largely ignore the rights of the customer. IBM is also in the unfortunate position of being the target for so many anti-trust actions that the company is understandably reluctant to risk any further legal problems by taking the lead that its position in the industry would seem to justify in negotiating Model Conditions of Contract.

In fairness to IBM, however, the following points should be mentioned:

Rental contract origins. For a number of reasons (not the least being the originally high cost of hardware and the rapid technical developments affecting early computers), the computer industry originally operated largely on a commercial rental basis. Indeed, until 1956, IBM equipment was available only on rental terms. Such contracts provide for a machine to be supplied to the customer in return for a periodic rental, and as long as the customer has the right to terminate the contract within a previously agreed period, and on giving reasonable notice, then the contract can be comparatively simple. There is no need for many of the normal purchase clauses such as those of the works, patents, designs, and copyrights, since property never passes to the customer. The customer is not committing himself to the expenditure of large capital sums, and can extricate himself from an unsatisfactory contract by simply giving notice of rental termination.

Such a contractual situation would seem to stack all the

cards against the manufacturer, but in practice this is not so. When any customer embarks on a computer-based operation, he does so in the expectation of improved efficiency or reduced cost (or both), and to achieve these objectives he will clearly need to phase out his manually operated system. As time goes on, he usually adds more to his computer-based system and thus becomes more and more dependent on it. So the ability to terminate a rental contract without cost is more apparent than real, particularly when the computer system is based on the hardware manufacturer's software application packages. To reinstate a manual system or to change the hardware and software to those supplied by another manufacturer can create a host of expensive difficulties.

Absence of customers' rights. The main problem with Conditions of Sale modeled on those of IBM is that, in extending the simple rental-contract philosophy to the purchase situation, manufacturers have ensured that they are protected against default by the customer, but have generally omitted giving similar protection to the customer against default by the manufacturer. The main criticism of the current Conditions of Sale used by most manufacturers must be not so much what they contain as what they omit. (Not that what is contained is perfect. For example, one clause usually included states that the contract is invalid unless signed by a duly authorized company representative. Just try to get a list of the "duly authorized representatives" and samples of their signatures to ensure that someone is not using the duly authorized representative's name and title in an unauthorized manner! Companies will no doubt tell you that they would honor the obligations of any contract that has gone through their administrative system, but why should they put the customer at any risk by inserting the clause at all?)

With the IBM kind of Conditions of Sale, the customer may suffer from the application of the contractual adage,

"What has not been written has not been said," The customer may still have his remedies in law, but it is extremely difficult to exercise them.

IBM's commercial leadership. As many computer manufacturers' Conditions of Sale are modeled after those of IBM, we now encounter a paradox. Almost anyone who has been involved in competitive bidding for computers where IBM is one of the competitors will know that IBM's price is often higher than that of many other manufacturers. It is generally accepted that IBM provides for resources to cover the backup services necessary for successful contracts (notwithstanding their lack of contractual promises). But without experience with smaller manufacturers and with no contractual assurances from them, it is difficult to make a comparative evaluation. Thus, in competition, IMB must suffer in relation to any manufacturer who excludes provisions for those backup services form his price.

There is one thing that cannot be in doubt: Manufacturers must firmly believe that Conditions of Contract or Conditions of Sale are necessary. Their insistence on their own conditions, which are written to give them adequate protection, demonstrates that they are not prepared to rely entirely on either commercial relationships or on litigation to ensure that they are protected.

MODEL CONDITIONS

There is often misunderstanding regarding the true intent and effect of Model Conditions of Contract. Many computer specialists argue that because of the complexity of computers, the interaction between systems, and the difficulty of measuring performances on equipment involving the use of software, it is impossible to formulate a Standard Contract. They are, of course, entirely correct, but the use of Model Conditions of Contract in no way implies any move toward a Standard Contract.

Model Conditions for the purchase of computer equipment are intended to provide a commercially equitable framework within which any variation of computer supply can be accommodated. None of the Conditions are intended to be mandatory, and if, for example, factory testing is not appropriate on a particular contract, then the Factory Testing Clause should be deleted. Similarly, If any unusual or unique agreement needs to be incorporated, then a clause can be added to reflect the agreement between the parties. The importance aspect of Model Conditions is that they provide an equitable base from which individual variations can be agreed upon by the contracting parties.

This seems a convenient point to draw a comparison between the commercial attitudes of the computer manufacturers and almost every other major industry. Differences arise which are reflected in attitudes toward Conditions of Contract, and these appear to stem from the fact that the computer industry is comparatively young and considers itself to be in a unique position in relation to conventional mechanical and electrical equipment: Software is usually quoted as the key difference.

If a buyer wishes to place a contract for the supply of almost any kind of equipment other than computers, there are recognized and accepted Model Conditions of Contract available.

Computer manufacturers have stated that they prefer to contract on the basis of their own Conditions of Sale, and most manufacturers will ignore a customer's conditions contained in his invitation to bid, and only quote on the basis of his own conditions. The main exceptions in the situation are where federal, state, and local government agencies are concerned. The extent to which government departments and large commercial organizations are successful in imposing their own Conditions of Contract on others depends almost entirely on the amount of commercial muscle they can exert. To be fair to the manufacturers, it must be said that many of the Conditions of Contract incorporated in invitations to bid are often quite inappropriate to computer contracts. The attitude of the computer manufacturers raises many problems which will be overcome only by the insistence by customers on the inclusion of clauses to protect their rights and by the recognition of the advantages that Model Conditions of Contract give. These include:

Brevity in documentation. When a set of Model Conditions is established and is readily available, there is no need to produce a complete set of conditions with every inquiry. Reference need only be made to the Model Form involved and to any variations (usually minimal) needed to meet individual contract requirements.

Basis in equity. Model Conditions should reflect the rights and obligations of both parties equally, and should not be biased in favor of either buyer or seller. The involvement of a reputable professional institute is the usual insurance in this situation.

Aid to evaluation. The evaluation of bids for complex computer systems is difficult enough from the purely technical angle without adding to the difficulties through commercial differences arising from various customers' and manufacturers' conditions.

Elimination of nonproductive examination and negotiation. The task of the examination and comparison of differing Conditions of Contract in the bid evaluation process is both time-consuming and difficult and, in the long run, it may cost many thousands of labor-hours, most of which are nonproductive. It is no use glossing over the small print if you are committing your organization to large sums of money, and the examination of conditions must be minute and thorough. If different conditions have been quoted by various manufacturers, these differences must be evaluated, and this is no easy task. Finally there is the negotiation relating to unacceptable conditions or for the addition of clauses which have been omitted.

Model Conditions are not put forward here as the panacea for all commercial problems, but they are undoubtedly an aid to the speedy placement of equitable contracts. There will always be situations where some condition required by one party is unacceptable to the other, and resolution of such problems will still be difficult, but mush time is wasted in reinventing the wheel. What happens so often is that a salesperson who does not understand the Conditions of Contract will come along to discuss and offer. When problems on Conditions are raised, he is unable to deal with them and refers them to a legal representative who understands the conditions but has no authority to change them. The final move is then to dicuss the matter with a senior executive who is authorized to make changes and is usually accompanied by the other two—an enormous waste of manpower! Thus, the expenditure of time on both sides is considerable, and much of it is spent on clauses where there are no fundamental differences between the parties, and it becomes a matter of agreement over terminology.

The situation just described presupposes that the customer has the expertise to conduct these negotiations successfully. In small companies there is often no one who can be spared to conduct such an exercise or, indeed, anyone with the specialized knowledge to undertake the negotiations. In these cases the customer often signs away his rights or, at best, make only marginal improvements in his contractual position.

2

Contract documentation

Where it is feasible to obtain competitive bids for equipment, this is the best course, but whether in competition or with a single supplier it is always advisable to get potential suppliers to quote against the stated requirements.

There is nothing to prevent anyone from inviting potential suppliers to discuss these requirements and asking them to produce solutions to the problem, but this usually means that the problem has not been identified. There must be any number of computer systems that have failed to satisfy the user and where the blame must lie on the user's shoulders for not knowing what he really wanted.

If a requirement is not specified accurately, no one can blame a manufacturer's representative for putting his own interpretation on the user's requirements and then offering the best solution that can be achieved from within his product range. There are two difficulties to be overcome in this situation. First, if the user cannot be specific and the explanation of his requirement is full of ambiguities, then the supplier will tend to concentrate on those aspects of the problem which he can solve, and the prime elements of the requirement may be overlooked. Secondly, if it is left to the manufacturers to interpret the requirement, it is almost inevitable that they will all interpret it in a slightly different way and the resulting bids will be almost impossible to compare with any degree of accuracy.

For the computer user, whether he be a first-time user or an existing user seeking to change his configuration, the first and prime requirement is to identify his needs and then write them down. This written document is the specification: It either details the user's needs as a description of the performance he requires (performance or workload specification) or details the equipment he needs to meet the performance that he has translated into equipment and softwave terms (technical or brand name or equivalent specification).

Performance or workload specification. A performance or workload specification can be written by someone who has no knowledge of computers, provided that he knows exactly what he wants to achieve. Against such a specification, the supplier is unconstrained in the choice of equipment and software he offers, and bids covering widely varying solutions may be received. If the potential user has no experience on which to judge these varying solutions, he will be at an obvious disadvantage in selecting the best offer, but he can include test criteria in the specification, and can require the supplier to demonstrate that the equipment or system meets the test criteria before he accepts it. One obvious problem in this area is that manual systems do not always convert easily or effectively into computerized systems. The author of a performance or workload specification who has no technical knowledge of computers and how to obtain the maximum benefit from them is at a serious disadvantage.

Technical specification or brand name or equivalent. The writing of a technical specification or the identification of brand-name or equivalent equipment is a job for an expert. He must know what the user requires and be able to translate that requirement into the computer hardware and software best suited for the job in relation to the available equipment, software packages, and latest developments in the computer industry.

The core of any computer contract is therefore the specification, and although "specification" is not a defined term in the Model Conditions (it is an extremely difficult term to define—it can mean so many things and take so many different forms), it is an integral part of any contract.

Just as a specification can take many forms, so can the inquiry and contract documentation. In this chapter, suggestions are given on points that may need to be covered, and a convenient form of presentation is demonstrated. The list is not exclusive, and any special requirements will need to be added.

COVERING LETTER

The covering letter, addressed to those firms being invited to submit a bid, is intended to detail the contents of the inquiry and to give covering information. The letter should be as short and concise as possible (the recipient must be able to read and understand it easily). It can normally be restricted to about six main points. Each of these has been discussed below.

Heading. This consist of a short but accurate description of the equipment or system for which bids are invited—for example, "Stores Control and Information Retrieval System" (the specification will give the scope and size of the requirement).

Introduction and content of the inquiry. This is a lead-in which invites the submission of a bid and goes on to detail the content of the bid documents that form part of the inquiry. These are usually:

> Customer's Instructions to Bidders
> Form of Bid and Appendixes (with blanks
>   to be filled in by the Contractor)
> Conditions of Contract
> Specification

This detailing ensures, among other things, that the prospective bidder is able to check that all documents have been included in his package.

Details for submission of bids. This usually states the number of copies of the bid that are required to be returned, where to return them (often under cover of a special label for identification purposes), and when the bid is due.

Contact for pre-bid inquiries. It is useful to nominate someone to deal with any pre-bid queries from bidders. This person should be named, and details should be provided about how he can be contacted.

Confirmation of receipt of inquiries. It is necessary to know that the inquiry has been received (in order to ensure that it has not gone astray in the mail) and that the firm will submit a bid. If a negative response is received quickly, there is usually still time to maintain the extent of competition by inviting a substitute bidder.

Bid reference. State the specific reference to be carried on all future correspondence relating to the inquiry. In a large organization, incoming mail improperly addressed can take a long time to reach the intended recipient or may not reach him at all.

A sample inquiry letter is shown in Appendix 2-1.

INSTRUCTIONS TO BIDDERS

In this document any general, nontechnical instructions need to be set out in detail, so that the bidder will know exactly what is required of him. Examples of the types of instruction usually found in this section are:

1. Details of the way in which the Form of Bid should be completed and whether variations in the Conditions of Contract or Specification will invalidate the offer.

2. Instructions regarding the way in which the bid is to be submitted (for example, in a sealed envelope or under cover of the special label).

3. In order to aid evaluation, bids are required on a common basis, and an instruction is usually included specifying that bids must be submitted strictly in accordance with the

Contract Documentation

inquiry and that any descriptive matter must support and not qualify the bid.

4. If, in addition to the main bid, alternatives will be considered, then this should be stated.

5. In order to ensure that there are no hidden extras to the bid price, it is common to instruct the bidders to include all incentives and bonuses and to state that no extra costs over and above the bid price will be admitted.

6. Detail any special instructions regarding legal, fiscal, or commercial legislation (such as federal, state, or local taxes).

7. Requirement on the recipients of the bid documents to treat the matter as confidential whether or not they submit a bid.

8. It is usual to reserve the right not to accept the lowest or any bid.

9. Unless there are exceptional circumstances, it is not usual to pay any expenses in relation to bid submission, in which case this ruling should be stated.

10. The requirement for bids to be submitted strictly in accordance with instructions can be reinforced by stating that any bid that does not comply may not be considered.

A sample of an "Instructions to Bidder" document is shown in Appendix 2-2.

FORM OF BID

This document is the formal declaration by the Contractor that he has examined the relevant documents and that in conformity with them he is prepared to carry out the work for the sum stated. It needs to be signed by a duly authorized representative of the bidding company.

As an appendix to the Form of Bid, there is often a program undertaking, which also needs to be completed and signed on behalf of the contractor.

A sample Form of Bid and Program Appendix is shown in Appendix 2-3.

CONDITIONS OF CONTRACT

This document consists of either the Conditions of Contract applicable to the inquiry or, if they are a readily available and published set of conditions, reference to them. Similarly, if the Customer's Conditions of Contract are well known to the Contractor, then reference only to them need be made.

In either case any amendments or additions to the Model Conditions need to be stated, together with details required for the Appendix to the Conditions.

A sample of the document detailing Conditions of Contract is shown in Appendix 2-4.

SPECIFICATION

This book is not intended to deal with the technical aspects of computing but, although the specification is essentially a technical document, there are a number of general requirements that are not specifically technical. A few examples of the types of headings typically used in a detailed specification might also be helpful.

General Requirements

Extent of contract. This is a statement of what is required (for example, supply only or supply, delivery, installation, and preparation for testing).

Installation information. If details of wiring and cabling installations, layout diagrams, or methods of fixing the equipment are required, then these should be stated.

Contractor's area. Where an area can be allocated to the Contractor or a storage room provided, details should be given.

Electrical requirements of the equipment. This is a statement of any regulations with which the Contractor must comply. It takes into account variations on normal mains supply phase and voltage within which the equipment must operate satisfactorily. Details of earthing requirements and requirements for cable connections are also included.

Environmental conditions. This involves confirmation that the customer will provide the necessary environmental conditions, details of which must be specified by the bidder in his offer (for example, total weight and size of equipment, required clearances, and operating temperature and air-change conditions).

Safety precautions. This spells out details of any site safety precautions that the Contractor's employees or his Subcontractors must observe.

Working conditions at premises. This is usually a statement that the Contractor is required to maintain the whole area of his operation in a clean, tidy, and safe condition.

Checking of work. This is a requirement for the Contractor to check all electrical and mechanical connections and to be responsible for correctness and safety.

Design and standards. This means either reference to specific standards or a general statement that American or other standards must be observed wherever applicable.

Subcontractors. This is a requirement that the Contractor submit a list of the principal Subcontractors he intends to employ.

Technical Requirements

No attempt will be made here to detail technical requirements, but any relevant publication—particularly by government bodies or qualified independent consultants—should be studied to ensure that requirements are properly specified. Some typical headings are:

Hardware– Processor, CRTs, printers, storage, communications.
Software– Language, calculations, updating, retrieval, sorting.

System reliability—Mean time between failures.
System availability—Mean time to repair.
Response time—Time for the system to respond.
Data entry—Method.
Data editing—Multiple edit features.
Information retrieval—Fields to be searched and output.

Once more it is stressed that specification writing is a highly skilled task and one that needs to be performed by a professional. The success of any project is dependent on the standard of the specification.

CONTRACT ACCEPTANCE

The contract acceptance letter should be unambiguous and unqualified; otherwise, it becomes a counter-bid, which in turn needs to be accepted by the Contractor. For example, if what is meant to be an acceptance letter states, "Your bid of _____ is accepted, except that your condition relating to the provision of documentation is rejected," then it is not an unqualified acceptance, but a counter-bid, and a contract does not exist until the recipient gives an unqualified acceptance of that counter-bid. There are times when a counter-bid has to be made (for example, where time constraints prevent the clearance of all outstanding queries), but this situation should be avoided whenever possible.

The acceptance letter should contain the following:

Heading—the same descriptive heading used in the inquiry should be followed through.

Acceptance statement—the formal statement of what is actually being accepted.

Contract price—a statement of the overall contract price and any details relating to it.

Contracting officer—the name of the Contracting Officer

Contract Documentation

and requirement that work should be carried out to his satisfaction.

Program of work—details of the commencement date of the contract and the date for its completion.

Conditions of contract—confirmation of the Conditions of Contract applicable to the contract.

Invoices and statutory charges—information on the way in which invoices should be submitted and how federal, state, and local taxes should be charged.

Acknowledgment—request for formal acknowledgment and confirmation that work is commencing. Also the name of the officer to whom all future correspondence should be addressed.

Contract reference—instruction that the contract reference must appear on all future correspondence.

A sample contract acceptance is shown in Appendix 2-5.

Appendix 2-1
Sample inquiry covering letter

To: _____
   _____
   _____

Gentlemen:

    Subject Heading_____

    Bid Reference _____

1. You are invited to submit a bid for the above work in accordance with the following Bid Documents:
    Customer's Instructions to Bidders
    Form of Bid and Appendix (all blanks to be filled in)
    Conditions of Contract
    Specification: General Requirements, Technical Requirements

2. One copy of the Bid Documents should be retained by you and the other _____ copies, completed as required, should be submitted to _____ under cover of the attached label, to arrive not later than _____. You are advised that the late bids may not be considered.

3. Any queries on technical matters should be addressed to _____ _____, telephone number _____.
All other queries should be referred to me at the address shown in the heading to this letter.

4. Please acknowledge receipt of this letter and accompanying documents, confirming that you will submit a bid by the due date.

5. All correspondence should quote the Bid Reference _____.

                        Sincerely yours,

                        _____

                        Name and Title

Contract Documentation

Appendix 2-2
Sample instructions to bidder

Bid Document _____

Bid Reference _____

1. The Form of Bid shall be signed, and all blanks in the Appendixes and Schedules shall be filled in as required. No alteration shall be made to the Form of Bid, Conditions of Contract, Specification, or other documents.

2. The bid shall be enclosed in a sealed cover endorsed and addressed as instructed in the inquiry covering letter and shall be delivered to the address specified not later than _____. The bidder shall submit the number of fully completed copies of the bid documents, with covering letter (if any) as required in the letter of inquiry.

3. The bidder is reminded that his basic offer should be strictly in accordance with the specification and other Bid Documents, and should not be qualified in any way. Any such qualification is liable to result in refusal to consider a bid which is otherwise favorable. The bidder should ensure, therefore, that any explanatory or descriptive matter included in his bid does not constitute a qualification to the requirements, terms, and conditions as stated in the inquiry documents.

4. If the bidder wishes to submit for consideration proposals on an alternative basis or bases, he will submit a bid in accordance with paragraph 3 above, and, in addition, submit the alternative proposed, with details of the omissions and additions which describe the alternative.

5. The bidder's particular attention is drawn to the fact that the Bid Price must cover all costs associated with labor, including the cost of any incentives necessary to attract and retain sufficient labor on site to meet the requirements of the program submitted in connection with the bid. The bidder's attention is further directed to the fact that the Bid Price must cover all increases in the cost of labor and materials

and that the Variations in Costs Clause in the Conditions of Contract will not form part of this contract.*

The submission of a bid shall be deemed to be an undertaking that the Bid Price covers the above.

6. The price quoted should include any federal, state, or local taxes, and shall be detailed in accordance with the legislation concerned.

7. Recipients of the Bid Documents (whether they submit a bid or not) shall treat the details of the documents as private and confidential.

8. The right is reserved not to accept the lowest or any bid, and the right is further reserved to accept the whole or part of any bid.

9. No payment will be made for any expenses or losses that may be incurred by any bidder in the preparation of his bid.

10. Any bid which does not conform to the foregoing instructions may not be considered.

*This assumes that a fixed price (i.e., not subject to the Variations in Costs Clause) is required. If a fixed price is not required, then this sentence should be deleted.

Appendix 2-3
Sample form of bid

Subject _____

Bid Reference _____

FORM OF BID

(*Note:* The Program Appendix forms part of the Bid)

To: (Customer's Name and Address) _____

_____

_____

Dear Sir:

Having examined the Conditions of Contract and Specification for the above-mentioned Works we, the undersigned, do hereby offer to carry out the said Works in conformity with the aforesaid Conditions of Contract and Specification for the fixed lump sum* of

_____

_____

Includes all taxes.

We hereby agree and undertake to complete the Works by the date shown in the attached Program Appendix to this Form of Bid.

We understand that the right is reserved not to accept the lowest or any bid that may be received.

Signed _____ Date _____

Name _____ Telephone Number _____

For and on behalf of _____ Telex Number _____

*This follows the logic of fixed price in Appendix 2.2 [For a definition of "Works," see Clause 1.15 in Chapter 4.]

SAMPLE PROGRAM APPENDIX TO FORM OF BID

Program and Time for Completion

Bid Document _____

Bid Reference _____

1. We understand that the Works are required to be delivered, installed, and completed by _____.

2. We understand that a Contract will be placed, or a letter of intention issued, on or about _____.

3. We, the undersigned, undertake to provide the equipment covered by this contract by the following dates:

(a) Completion of Works Tests and delivery within _____ weeks of acceptance of our bid.

(b) Completion of installation within _____ weeks of delivery.

(c) Completion of Acceptance Tests within _____ weeks of installation.

Signed _____ Date _____

For and on behalf of _____

Appendix 2-4
Sample document—conditions of contract

Bid Document _____

Bid Reference _____

The Conditions of Contract shall be the (make reference to published Model Conditions or to the set of Conditions enclosed) _____

Clause 11.2. Time the essence of the contract. This clause is deleted, since time is not the essence of the contract.

Clause 12. Factory tests. This clause is deleted, since factory tests are not required.

Clause 20. Variations in costs. * This clause is deleted and the Contract Price will therefore be firm and not subject to adjustment on account of increases or decreases in the cost and price of labor and materials.

Appendix to the conditions. (Figures to be inserted.)

*Once more the logic of fixed price in Appendix 2-2 is followed.

Appendix 2-5
Sample contract acceptance

To: _____
_____
_____

Gentlemen:

Subject Heading _____

Contract Reference _____

Your bid dated _____, submitted in response to my inquiry letter dated _____, is accepted, for the supply, delivery, installation, testing, and setting to work of _____ _____ in the Computing Center at _____ _____.

The Contract Price is _____($_____), which is a fixed lump sum inclusive of all labor, materials, packing, transportation, and all other costs and taxes.

The work under the contract shall be undertaken in accordance with the Bid Document Reference _____ dated _____ and to the satisfaction of the Contracting Officer who shall be _____ at _____.

The commencement date of the contract is the date of this letter. Delivery, installation, testing, and setting to work shall be completed within _____ weeks of that date.

The Conditions of Contract shall be the (make reference to published Model Conditions or to the set of Conditions enclosed with the inquiry) _____, modified as detailed in form headed Conditions of Contract in the Bid Document Reference _____.

Please send your acknowledgment of this letter to me, notifying your acceptance of the contract and confirming that the work has commenced in accordance with the terms and conditions set out herein. Thereafter, all correspondence in connection with the execution of the contract, except as otherwise requested, shall be addressed to the Contracting Officer.

All invoices and future correspondence should quote the Contract Reference _____.

       Sincerely yours,

      (Name)_____
      (Title)_____

3

Small and first-time users

For the experienced buyer, the concept of Model Conditions will not be new and the IPS Model Conditions for the purchase of computer equipment will, it is hoped, be an additional aid in his normal purchasing activities. The Conditions themselves and the explanatory notes should enable such people to cover all the commercial aspects of computer purchasing, and they will have adequate technical backup, or at least will know where such backup can be found.

For the first-time user—and even for the small user who already has some experience of computing and now wishes either to revise or to enhance his equipment—the situation is somewhat more difficult. To be presented with a set of conditions to enable an equitable commercial deal to be negotiated is only a part, and perhaps a comparatively small part, of the total task of getting a computerized system.

It is not the purpose of this book to deal with the technical aspects of choosing a computer system, and the Model Conditions alone will be of little use to the uninformed buyer without some information on the context within which they need to be used. This section has therefore been designed to give additional information specifically to assist small and first-time users.

ASSESSING THE NEED

It may seem fairly obvious that an objective assessment must be made of the need to introduce a computerized system, but there are numerous stories about companies becoming computer users because "computers must be a good thing, so many people have them," or merely to "keep up with the Joneses." One of the problems with a computerized system is that if you start off on the wrong foot, you tend to get caught up in an enhancement loop that can cost a great deal of money while not necessarily obtaining the facility required.

The first requirement, therefore, is to examine the company as it stands and ask the questions, "What are we doing?"; "Where are we going?"; "Are we profitable?"; and so on. This means taking a close look at the objectives and activities of the company and the commercial environment in which it operates, and assessing the strengths and weaknesses of the company's position. With many small firms, all of these things may be obvious to the management, but it pays to stand back and take stock before making such a major move as introducing a computerized system.

Once the objectives and direction of the company have been determined, the next requirement is to examine the internal structure of the company in relation to those objectives. The objective may be to raise the level of profitability by reducing operating costs, in which case a possible reduction in personnel may be an important aspect in the introduction of a computerized system. On the other hand, if it is desired to streamline modes of operation and improve information flow in order to achieve better customer service, then the priorities are obviously different, and a reduction in costs may not be the first priority. Here again, with many small firms, a formal analysis may not be necessary, but management should take a little time, even in an operational area that they know intimately, to ensure that they know where their priorities lie.

The analysis requires an examination of the performance of the company—in past, current, and future terms—in relation to the manual systems in operation at the moment.

This will help determine whether a computer can assist in meeting the objectives. As a result of this examination, the conclusion may be reached that some rationalization or restructuring without the use of computers will achieve these objectives, but if the final decision is to computerize, then the following points should be considered.

JUSTIFICATION FOR COMPUTERIZATION

What is required here is a costed feasibility study. One of the problems in carrying out this type of study is understanding what a computer can offer a company. Because this is a technical problem, a consulting firm should be employed. Without the advantage of independent professional advice, the prospective user has two alternatives open to him: He can either make his own assessment of the benefits of computerization with the help of whatever expertise is available within the company; or he can call in a computer manufacturer and ask him to advise on a system. In that case, any computer manufacturer would be delighted to assist, and if the user is lucky he will have selected a reputable company that has the right kind of computers, operating software, and experience for his company, and he may end up with a very good system. On the other hand, the computer manufacturer is unlikely to recommend that the company look to one of his competitors, even where his own equipment and experience is not entirely suited to the user's requirements. The manufacturer is more likely to try to sell his own equipment and to get the user to tailor his requirements to meet the computer system he is marketing.

In the absence of the necessary expertise within the company, by far the best course is to employ independent qualified professional consultants. The consultant should not be connected in any way with any specific manufacturer, and, therefore, should not be under commercial pressure to sell hardware. Specifically, the consultant will carry out assignments to assess the feasibility of having a computer, to help select equipment you need, and to help implement the assignment.

Bearing in mind the company's established objectives, an evaluation of the costs, benefits, and consequences of installing a computerized system needs to be made. This evaluation may start with an initial consideration of computerized alternatives in those areas of the management system where problems are currently being experienced and where benefits are most likely to be achieved but could extend to a computerized system covering all of the firm's activities. It would, however, be a bold firm that would be prepared to switch suddenly to a completely computerized system.

The first phase of the evaluation is unlikely to establish more than a crude measure of the costs or benefits involved and the type of equipment likely to meet the user's requirements. This should, however, be an adequate basis on which the senior management of the company can be consulted, to obtain a directive authorizing detailed appraisal of alternative systems. This in turn should lead to a recommended system solution, but without any commitment as to the type of equipment required.

As part of these considerations, it is essential that company management consider all the consequences of the recommended system, particularly its impact on staff. At this time it might be advisable to consult with staff or union representatives on the projected development and how this will affect the staff concerned. There is no need to emphasize the importance of good industrial relations, and it must always be kept in mind that the introduction of computers can mean a considerable change in staffing structures. A computer has its own requirements for specialized staff, but on the other hand, the preparation of a great deal of the computer input data is a very routine operation. Existing staff people qualified in other professions are unlikely to want to be involved in this routine activity, but they must be informed of the benefits of a computer in relieving professional staff people of routine work. Information flow is aided and the professional can spend more time on professional activities rather than on evolving and working laborious manual systems.

COMPETITION AMONG ALTERNATIVE SYSTEMS

Assuming that all the cost-benefit analyses have been carried out, that any potential industrial relations problems have been cleared, and that the system has been specified, the next problem is how to choose your system from among the many available ones. Here again is an area where independent expertise is extremely valuable, if not essential.

The first task is to review the market in relation to the system specification and to establish who produces the type and size of computer required. Additionally, consideration should be given to contractors who operate a "turnkey" operation—those who will supply a complete system and set it to work as part of an overall contract (at a cost)—and to software houses that may have specialist packages which would ideally suit customer needs.

When the range of equipment, software, and contractual options has been established, then a request for proposals should be issued to those firms who can meet the selected system requirements. This is another job which ideally should be done by a professional, since the content of the request obviously determines the basis of the bids received and must incorporate a very firm specification of requirements. Having "sized" the system requirements, the specification should be able to detail the type of machine, the type of software, the application to which the equipment and software will be put, the volumes of work to be handled, and the response times that are required. This is the document that determines the technical response from the Contractor.

The remainder of the invitation to bid documentation should contain any special commercial instructions, such as to whom the offer should be addressed, any particular date and time by which it must be received, and whom to contact in case of difficulties. Reference must be made to the Conditions of Contract. Because the main purpose of this book is related to the Conditions, no further details will be given here, but it is stressed that the Conditions are framed in such a way as to ensure that both the customers' and the manufacturers' interests are protected, and the customer should insist that the Contractor quote to them. It is not necessary to enclose a copy of the Model Conditions with the bid invitation, if they are known to the Contractor, but merely to make reference to them. However, if any additions or deletions are to be introduced into the Conditions, then it should be made clear what these are.

Selection of the System

The appraisal of bids is a very difficult task; once again, it is best handled by professionals. Most computer manufacturers are very skilled in presenting glossy, persuasive offers, and since a user's priority should be to get the best price-performance ratio, then it needs somebody to cut through the glossy surface and get down to the real content of the bid.

There is no easy answer to the question of how to ensure a proper evaluation of bids; it is a detailed exercise that calls for considerable expertise. The technical experts will obviously take account of the price-performance ratios, the type of equipment, and its potential for future development. Here it must be remembered that the workload of virtually every computer system installed increases rapidly once the benefits are appreciated, and a system that will meet the user's needs today is not necessarily the best system for the future. Some systems are modular and can be extended by simple additions; others have memory constraints or limitations on the number of work stations that can be accommodated, and there are so many other aspects for technical evaluation that expert technical assistance is strongly recommended.

In the commercial evaluation, costs are a prime consideration. But it is a mistake always to expect the cheapest to be the best value, and hidden costs such as repetitive costs of software packages, the cost of maintenance in relation to user requirements (for example, periodic or on call), the cost of installation and environmental requirements (some computers need air conditioning), the question of when payments start, and all the other commercial aspects need to be evaluated and combined with the technical considerations.

INSTALLATION AND PREPARATION FOR TESTING

Having selected the computer manufacturer and placed the contract, it is quite usual for the technical consultant to be involved only on a periodic basis from this stage, but there are a number of requirements that should by now have been planned.

The first essential is to ensure that an implementation plan between the computer manufacturer and the user is agreed upon and that a system of project control is implemented. Periodic progress meetings need to be organized, and lines of communication both within the company and with the manufacturer need to be established.

The man in charge of the project will obviously have to ensure that any alterations to the site are carried out and that any special environmental conditions necessary are provided before the computer is delivered. The required type of continuous stationery and other computer consumables, such as magnetic tapes and disks, needs to be established, and supplies must be arranged so that they are available by the installation date. During this period, it is also essential to ensure that the user departments within the company are aware of progress and what the system will provide when it is operational. This aspect is important, since it is only too easy to think that other people know what is going on in your own mind; they do not, and oral communication is often erratic. Some form of progress bulletin is very helpful in this respect. It is also during this period that training of staff needs to begin, and manufacturers will often provide facilities for staff to attend courses and use their equipment in order to get "hands on" experience.

When it comes to implementation, it is usual to have a period of parallel operation, with the old manual system and the new computerized system running concurrently, in order to ensure that the computerized system is adequate and efficient before the old manual system is discontinued. It is often helpful to introduce the computer system section by section, rather than all at once as a total operation, since initial implementation problems will undoubtedly occur. However, the overall payoff with respect to computer usage is high, and despite much uninformed criticism regarding the use of computers, there are few cases where users would be prepared to revert to manual operation once their computerized system has been proved and is working effectively. It must be remembered, however, that a computer system is only as good as the information fed into it, and failure to produce the required results is more often the fault of the user than of the computer—again provided that the right system has been chosen.

Professional bodies, management organizations, and consultants often run seminars and workshops to meet the needs of prospective computer users. An application to any of these will secure the information you require in order to arrange training for those people on whom you will depend for a smooth transition from manual to computerized operation.

4

Model form of conditions of contract for the supply and installation (purchase) of computer equipment

This section constitutes the core of the book. The text of each clause in the Institute's Model Conditions is set out in full, and is followed by an explanation and comments designed to enable the buyer to use the Conditions sensibly and effectively.

Workable contracts must represent the intent of both parties and must therefore be written in a way that truly reflects those intentions and leaves no room for ambiguities. Clearly it is essential to understand the effect of introducing these contractual clauses, but it is equally essential to know how they should be applied and to be able to recognize the rights and obligations of the parties, as well as the limitations that they impose.

The Model Conditions represent the varied experience of many people who have been involved in the technical aspects and purchase of computer equipment over a number of years. One point they all stress is that the key to all successful contracts is the necessity for both parties to act reasonably.

If both parties adopt a reasonable attitude toward the interpretation and application of contract requirements, then commercial harmony will usually result. The fact that a clause gives the right to take a certain action does not, of course, make it obligatory to take that action and, depending on the circumstances, it might even be better to relax the requirement, particularly where the other party is doing his best and where the application of the rights under a clause is unlikely to produce long-term benefits.

The inclusion of equitable conditions in a contract is often sufficient in itself to induce a reasonable attitude because, in the event of difficulties, the rights of both parties are clearly established. If either party adopts a recalcitrant attitude, then the conditions enable the other party to obtain his rights, provided he knows how to go about exercising them.

The Institute of Purchasing Model Conditions were produced for use in the United Kingdom, and in their original form certain clauses are not entirely applicable to American commercial practices and terminology. Where simple changes can reflect American practices, these alterations have been made, but where the American practices are diverse or are not precisely known, the original British text has been retained and additional notes have been added to cover the American requirements.

Model Form of Conditions of Contract

Synopsis of model form of conditions of contract

CLAUSE	TITLE	CLAUSE	TITLE
1	Definitions	20	Variations in Costs
2	Contractor to Inform Himself Fully	21	Ownership
		22	Recovery of Sums Due
3	Standard of the Works		
4	The Premises	23	Warranty Period
5	Drawings	24	Bankruptcy
6	Mistakes in Information	25	Statutory and Other Regulations
7	Program of Works		
8	Delivery and Installation	26	Waiver
9	Variations	27	Confidentiality
10	Extension of Time for Completion	28	Consumable Supplies
		29	Maintenance
11	Delays	30	Spares
12	Factory Tests	31	Software
13	Acceptance Tests	32	Force Majeure
14	Acceptance Certificate	33	Attachments to the Equipment
15	Patents, Designs, and Copyright		
		34	Training
16	Standard of Performance	35	Publicity
17	Assignment and Subletting	36	Operating Manuals
18	Indemnity and Insurance	37	Arbitration
19	Terms of Payment	38	Law

CLAUSE 1. DEFINITIONS
1.1 "Acceptance Date" shall be the date certified by the Contracting Officer as the date when the Works passed the Acceptance Tests and were ready for operational use. [For a definition of "Works," see clause 1.15.]

1.2 "Completion Date" shall mean the date included in the Contract or, where not so specified, the date included in the Program of Works as the date upon which the Works are to be ready for operational use.

1.3 "Contract" shall mean the agreement between the Customer and the Contractor for the execution of the Works, including all documents to which reference may properly be made in order to ascertain the rights and obligations of the parties.

1.4 "Contractor" shall mean the person, firm, or company whose offer has been accepted by the Customer and shall include the Contractor's personal representatives, successors, and permitted assigns.

1.5 "Contract Price" shall mean that sum so named in the Contract together with any additions thereto or deductions therefrom agreed in writing under the Contract.

1.6 "Customer" shall mean_____
and shall include the Customer's legal personal representatives, successors, and assigns.

1.7 "Equipment" shall mean all materials, plant, and hardware supplied by the Contractor, including basic-level machine control facilities, for inclusion in the Works.

1.8 "Factory Tests" shall mean the tests included in the Contract to be carried out prior to delivery to ensure that the Equipment and Software comply with the specified requirements.

1.9 "Premises" shall mean the place or places other than the Contractor's premises to which the Equipment and Software are to be delivered or where work is to be done.

1.10 "Program of Works" shall mean the timing and sequence of events agreed between the Customer and the Contractor for the performance of the Contract.

1.11 "Software" shall mean all operating systems, compilers, utilities, service software, and other programs and associated documentation provided by the Contractor for inclusion in the Works.

1.12 "Subcontractor" shall mean any person (other than the Contractor) named in the Contract for any part of the Works or any person to whom any part of the Contract has been (with

Model Form of Conditions of Contract 41

the consent in writing of the Customer) sublet, and the legal representatives, successors, and permitted assigns of such person.

1.13 "Contracting Officer" shall mean the person temporarily or occasionally appointed by the Customer and notified in writing to the Contractor, to act as the Customer's representative for the purpose of the Contract or, in default of such notification, the customer.

1.14 "Acceptance Tests" shall mean the tests included in the Contract and/or such other tests as may be agreed in writing between the Customer and the Contractor to be carried out by the Contractor after delivery to the Premises and before the Acceptance Date.

1.15 "Works" shall mean and include the supply, delivery, installation, testing, and setting to work of the Equipment and Software and all other work required to be carried out by the Contractor under the Contract.

EXPLANATORY NOTES

There are two reasons for including a list of definitions in Model Conditions. First, it ensures that every time a term is used, it is easily recognized and identified with a specific meaning. For example, every time reference is made to the Contractor, the first letter is upper case and it always means, "the person, firm, or company whose offer has been accepted by the Customer, and shall include the Contractor's personal representatives, successors, and permitted assigns." Thus there is no ambiguity as to who can legally act in that capacity. Secondly, it saves repeating the meaning in full every time and avoids the danger of slight changes in wording resulting in differences of meaning that were never intended. One would not expect there to be many problems in identifying the Contractor, but when it is necessary to apply responsibilities and obligations relating to the "Works," the "Equipment," and the "Software," it is necessary that the Model Conditions leave no room for misunderstanding.

None of the definitions need further explanation regarding the meaning of the terms (it is the purpose of the definition to provide that explanation), but some background to the inclusion of some of the definitions and the reasons for the restriction of certain matters is essential for a proper understanding of the clauses in which the terms are used.

Before dealing with individual definitions, there is one general convention in Model Conditions that needs to be mentioned: Words in the singular or plural are interchangeable within the context of the clause. This eliminates the need to use alternatives such as "his/their," "item(s)," and so on, which would make reading and understanding unnecessarily difficult.

"Acceptance Date" (Clause 1.1)

Payments are initiated by issuing an Acceptance Certificate, but the date of the issue of that certificate is often later than the Acceptance Date. This should only be a result of the mechanics of actually issuing the certificate, and the Customer is not entitled to delay the issue of the certificate unreasonably once the Works have passed the Acceptance Tests and are ready for operational use.

"Completion Date" (Clause 1.2)

The importance of this date is that it is the date when the Customer requires that the Works be completed and ready for his use. It is, therefore, of prime importance to him, and it is highly desirable that this date be specified precisely before the contract is placed and that it form part of the contract documentation. Unfortunately circumstances can occur where a Customer wants to use the Works as early as possible, but where at the time of placing the contract the Contractor can only specify completion within a period—for example, completion by the end of the second quarter of a year. This means that the Contractor discharges his obligations if he completes them by June 30 of that year, but when the Program of Works is developed, it will demonstrate why the inclusion of a detailed "Completion Date" in the contract documentation is important: It is the key to the operation of Clause 10 (Extension of Time for Completion) and Clause 11 (Delays). Without a clearly defined "Completion Date," it is difficult to control the effect of delays by either party and to obtain appropriate redress from the party in default.

"Contract" (Clause 1.3)

An initial requirement is to withdraw in writing any Conditions that are not applicable to any specific contract and to supplement them if there are any special additional needs. Ideally, contract documentation should be kept to a minimum and made as simple as possible. Where it is necessary to refer to exchange of correspondence, notes of meeting, written undertakings, and so on, it is useful to schedule these as an attachment to the contract acceptance. This can often save subsequent arguments regarding what is—or is not—a contractual obligation.

"Contractor" (Clause 1.4)

A "permitted assign" is someone to whom permission has been granted, by the other party to a Contract, for the transfer of rights or obligations, or both.

"Equipment" (Clause 1.7)

What is described as "Equipment" is basically the physical components of a computer installation. This is the traditional description of hardware, but with the current development of "built-in" software, it was believed that another term was needed to embrace the basic-level machine control facilities.

"Factory Tests" (Clause 1.8)

In most cases the Customer will buy a standard product and will rely on the manufacturer's description of the equipment and software in order to run Acceptance Tests on his own installation. In normal circumstances, therefore, this subclause and Clause 12 should be deleted.

"Premises" (Clause 1.9)

If the Contractor is to perform work on the Customer's premises, it is essential that he be given either facilities to inspect the premises, or adequate information to enable him to take account of (and price for) all physical and environmental factors.

"Program of Works" (Clause 1.10)

If the Customer requires sequential completion of the Works, this should be clearly specified in the invitation to bid. Difficulties can arise if a requirement for sequential completion is introduced after the Contract is placed, since the Contractor will then have already priced the alternatives on the basis of his own program for meeting the final Completion Date.

"Software" (Clause 1.11)

Because of developments in the area of operating systems and other systems software, it is necessary for this to be separated from "Equipment" and defined separately as well. The words "other programs" have been used to permit the inclusion in the Contract of the supply of "application" packages by the Contractor.

"Contracting Officer" (Clause 1.13)

The Customer is usually a company or a large organization, and confusion can occur in the day-to-day relationships between the employees or representatives of both the Customer and Contractor unless it is clearly established who is entitled to issue instructions and take actions on behalf of the Customer. For this reason, the Contracting Officer should be appointed and notified to the Contractor as soon as possible after the placing of the Contract.

"Acceptance Tests" (Clause 1.14)

With most standard equipment, the Contractor will include in his catalog pricing the cost of his normal Acceptance Tests. The Customer should ensure that these tests would be sufficient for his purposes and, if not, he must specify what further Acceptance Tests are needed, bearing in mind that these may well cost extra.

CLAUSE 2. CONTRACTOR TO INFORM HIMSELF FULLY

The Contractor shall be deemed to have examined the Premises, the requirements specified, and these Conditions. No claim from the Contractor for additional payment will be allowed on the grounds of misinterpretation of any matter relating to the Premises, the requirements specified, or these Conditions on which the Contractor could reasonably have satisfied himself by a visit to the Premises, reference to the Contracting Officer, or such other means as may be appropriate.

EXPLANATORY NOTES

Problems can, and do, arise where the Contractor does not adopt the simple expedient of examining the premises where his equipment is to be delivered. What happens if the equipment is too large to get through the computer-room doorway? Who should pay the cost if structural alterations are necessary? Or perhaps structural alterations are impossible for operational reasons: In that event, has the Customer the right to return the equipment, and if so, has he the right of cancellation? Who pays any resulting costs?

Without a clear understanding of the obligations of each of the parties to a contract, such matters can result in deteriorating relationships, protracted negotiations, and even litigation (in extreme cases). This clause makes it clear where the obligation lies in all matters relating to the Premises.

It might be thought that a clause which puts all the obligation for finding out about the Customer's Premises onto the Contractor is unfair to him, but this is not so. When a Customer issues a request for proposals, he is usually unaware of the details of all the equipment that the Contractor is likely to propose to meet his requirements, or of any supplementary equipment needed for installation and testing, and so on. It is, therefore, up to the Contractor to include in his bid all costs associated with the provision of his equipment and to stipulate what environmental conditions and access facilities he requires.

A further reason for the inclusion of this clause is to aid the Customer in evaluating offers. The cost of an installation to a Customer must include all structural alterations and environmental provisions in his Premises, and he must know what these requirements are in order to cost them and to perform a true comparative evaluation. It can come as a painful shock to a DP manager if, after doing all his cost-benefit analyses on a new installation, he is suddenly confronted with a large bill for structural alterations.

Needless to say, facilities for the bidders to visit the Premises must be granted by the Customer. Arrangements should be detailed in the invitation to bid, including the nomination of the Contracting Officer.

CLAUSE 3. STANDARD OF THE WORKS
The Works shall be in accordance with the Contract. To the extent that the Standard of the Works has not been specified in the Contract, the Contractor shall use good quality materials, techniques, and standards, and shall execute the Contract with the care, skill, and diligence required in accordance with best computing practice.

EXPLANATORY NOTES

The establishment of standards in the computing industry is currently the subject of much debate. It is beyond the intent of this book to make any technical statements on this matter, but the Customer naturally wants to ensure that the best practices and materials have been employed in the manufacture of the Equipment and Software he is purchasing.

For this reason, the informed Customer will keep up to date with the latest technical developments, and will specify those standards that the manufacturer must observe. But even he will never be sure that he is completely up to date and has covered all developments.

The situation for the man who is just entering the computer area is much more difficult, since he will probably know little about computer technology, and small firms may not wish—or be able—to employ experts on a permanent basis.

Therefore, this clause is written in general terms to protect the Customer against second-rate practices and materials being used by the Contractor. In the event of unsatisfactory performance by the Contractor or by his Equipment or Software, however, the onus will be on the Customer to prove that the Contractor is in default.

CLAUSE 4. THE PREMISES
4.1 *Preparation and Provision.*
4.1.1 The Contractor shall in his bid supply adequate information to enable the Customer to prepare the Premises for the Works and to provide:
(i) A suitable supply of electric current and such other main services;
(ii) All other required electrical and mechanical items and fittings (other than the Equipment and Software);
(iii) Such environmental conditions as are necessary for the purposes of the Works.

4.1.2 The Customer, at his own expense, shall ensure that such preparation and provision are made in accordance with the Program of Works. In the event that such preparation and provision are unsuitable for the purpose of the Works as the result of an act or default of one party, then any reasonable costs thereby incurred by the other party shall be recoverable.

4.2 *Access.*

4.2.1 The Contracting Officer shall afford to the authorized personnel of the Contractor, at all reasonable times and with prior agreement, such access to the Premises (but not necessarily sole access) as may be necessary for the inspection thereof and for the execution of the Works, provided always that the Contracting Officer shall have the right to refuse admittance to, or order the removal from, the Premises of any person employed by or acting on behalf of the Contractor or Subcontractor who in the opinion of the Contracting Officer is not a fit and proper person to be on the Premises. (In these matters, the opinion of the Contracting Officer shall be final.) Action taken under this clause shall forthwith be confirmed in writing to the Contractor by the Contracting Officer, and shall not relieve the Contractor of his obligations under the Contract.

4.2.2 In the event that the Contractor is not provided with sole access to the Premises, the Contractor must take reasonable care to ensure that in the execution of the Works he does not interfere with the operations of the Customer, his employees, or any other contractor employed on the Premises.

EXPLANATORY NOTES

"Preparation and Provision" (Clause 4.1)

This is another clause designed to remove ambiguity, this time from the type of situation where the Customer fails to provide adequate services or to prepare the Premises for the installation of the Contractor's equipment. If the Contractor arrives at the Customer's Premises and finds that the facilities needed to install his equipment have not been provided, there will inevitably be delay. There could also be an argument over who should have provided what, and who will be responsible for any additional costs that may arise.

The clause clearly requires the Contractor to state what services and environmental conditions are required, and stipulates that it is the Customer's responsibility to provide them. If this sounds like an invitation to the Contractor to ask for excessive provisions, it must be remembered that as part of the comparison of costs of one bid against another made by the Customer, his own costs for the provisions made on his premises will be included.

Because of the obligations and responsibilities that this clause places on both parties, it is obvious that either party could default and cause the other party to incur additional costs. In such cases, the defaulting party must bear the additional costs, but it is the obligation of the injured party to take all reasonable steps to keep such costs to a minimum.

"Access" (Clause 4.2)

Access to the Customer's Premises can cause problems, particularly if there are security-related or confidentiality-related constraints affecting the Contractor's freedom of access for inspection, installation, and so on. Any special regulations or procedures must therefore be stated by the Customer in his invitation to bid, and the Contractor will have to consider the effect that restriction of working hours, the introduction of special working permits, or other procedures will have on his costs, and ensure that he provides for them in his bid price.

Problems can also arise out of the purely mechanistic aspect of ensuring that only "authorized personnel of the Contractor" are given access to the Customer's Premises. If, for security reasons, the Contractor has to put his employees through a screening process, this must be done, because access will only be granted to employees with the agreed-upon documentation to prove they are properly authorized. Once more, the Customer must make his requirements known in the invitation to bid to enable the Contractor to allow for these extra costs in his bid price.

A further point on access is the reference to the finality of the Contracting Officer's decision on whether a person employed by, or acting on behalf of, the Contractor is not "a fit and proper person to be on the Premises." The inclusion of this right for the Contracting Officer is necessary, and he must be in a position to apply the right without any time-consuming formalities. Imagine the damage a drunken Contractor's employee could do if he could not be removed immediately from the Customer's Premises! A Customer's employee in the same condition could do an equal amount of damage, but that is the Customer's responsibility.

Another important point is that the Contractor may not always have sole access to the Premises, in which case he must ensure that he does not interfere with other operations that are taking place concurrently.

CLAUSE 5. DRAWINGS
5.1 The Contractor shall submit to the Customer for approval within the time specified in the Contract (or, if no time is specified, such time as will enable the Program of Works to be maintained) drawings as may be detailed or required for the purpose of the Contract.
5.2 Within a reasonable period after receiving such drawings, the Customer shall signify his approval or otherwise. If the Customer requires changes to be made to any drawing submitted for approval, the same shall forthwith be modified by the Contractor to meet the requirements of the Customer and then be resubmitted for approval. The approval of drawings shall not relieve the Contractor from his obligations to execute the Works in accordance with the Contract.

Model Form of Conditions of Contract 51

5.3 Drawings approved as described in Subclause 5.2 shall not be departed from except as provided for in Clause 9 (Variations).

EXPLANATORY NOTES

Whereas the Customer is required to approve such design, manufacturing, installation, interconnection, and dimensional detail drawings as are required under the Contract, it behooves the Customer to require only such drawings as are necessary. Contractors usually have a standard package of documentation, including drawings for their standard models, and will be prepared to supplement these with such layout details and other items that are necessary. But they will rightly charge extra for requirements in excess of what they consider to be normal for the type of installation involved.

Both parties should ensure that requirements and costs are detailed before the Contract is completed. Much bad feeling can be generated if either party believes the other is being unreasonable when requirements have not previously been specified by one or accepted by the other.

The other point to note in relation to this clause is that approval of the drawings by the Customer does not relieve or alter the Contractor's obligation to execute the Works in accordance with the Contract. The rationale for this item is that responsibility for final performance cannot be divided and that the Contractor is—and must accept that he is—the expert where his own equipment is concerned. If the Customer insists on alternatives which the Contractor considers would jeopardize the performance of his equipment, then he must obtain a waiver of performance from the Customer for that aspect where he considers performance would be affected.

CLAUSE 6. MISTAKES IN INFORMATION

6.1 The Contractor shall be responsible for, and shall pay extra costs occasioned by, any discrepancies, errors, or omissions in drawings, documentation, or other information supplied in writing by him, whether they have been approved by the Customer or not, provided that such discrepancies, errors, or omissions are not the result of inaccurate drawings or information and decisions supplied in writing to the Contractor by the Customer.

6.2 The Customer shall be responsible for, and shall pay any extra costs directly occasioned by, and discrepancies, errors, or omissions in the drawings, information, and decisions supplied in writing to the Contractor by the Customer.

EXPLANATORY NOTES

It is common sense that any additional costs arising from mistakes, discrepancies, errors, and omissions in any drawings, information, or decisions supplied by one party to the other should be met by the party in default, and it is unlikely that any court would take a contrary view. However, it is not unknown for a defaulting party to deny this obligation. In that case, recourse to litigation can be a costly and protracted business.

This clause makes absolutely clear the obligations and responsibilities of both parties, and it should eliminate any arguments regarding liability in principle. It will still be for the injured party, seeking reimbursement of additional costs, to demonstrate the costs that have been incurred over and above what would have been occasioned had the default not occurred, and to demonstrate that all reasonable steps had been taken to minimize them.

CLAUSE 7. PROGRAM OF WORKS

7.1 The Contractor shall include in his bid an outline Pro-

Model Form of Conditions of Contract

gram of Works to meet the specified Completion Date, and, within 21 days of the Customer's authorization to proceed (or such other period as may be agreed), shall submit to the Contracting Officer for his approval a detailed program showing the number of days or weeks required for each separate stage to ensure that the Works are ready for operational use by the Completion Date.

7.2 On receipt of the detailed program, the Contracting Officer shall:
(i) Signify his approval of the program; *or*
(ii) Reject the program, stating his reasons for so doing, and require that the program be amended by the Contractor. The Contracting Officer's approval or rejection of the Contractor's detailed program (or amended program) shall be notified to the Contractor within a time scale that reflects the total program time available to the Contractor to carry out the Contract.

EXPLANATORY NOTES

This is essentially a practical clause in that it requires the initial submission of an outline Program of Works with the Contractor's bid and then the submission, for approval by the Customer, of a detailed program showing the time required for each separate stage of the Works.

The outline program is required by the Customer so that he can judge the practicability of the Contractor's proposals in relation to his own requirements, which may include temporarily shutting down or moving his existing installation. If this outline broadly meets his requirements and a Contract results, he must then have this outline plan converted to a detailed program to enable him to make his arrangements for meeting the Contractor's environmental requirements and providing the necessary services, as well as making any necessary arrangements for continued operation during the installation period.

CLAUSE 8. DELIVERY AND INSTALLATION

8.1 No Equipment or Software may be delivered to the Premises without the prior permission of the Contracting Officer. The Contractor shall be responsible for the delivery of the Equipment and Software to all Premises, and shall receive them thereon and shall provide all labor, materials, and plant required for the off-loading and placing in position of the Equipment and Software, and for all other purposes of the Contract. The Contractor shall be responsible for the safe custody of the Equipment and Software and his other equipment until the Acceptance Date, after which the Contractor shall remove his other equipment, leaving the Premises and the Works clean and ready for operational use.

8.2 The Contractor may work on the Premises only with the authorization of the Contracting Officer.

EXPLANATORY NOTES

This clause starts with a clear instruction to the Contractor that he must not deliver Equipment or Software to the Customer's Premises without the prior permission of the Contracting Officer. There have been occasions when expensive and vulnerable equipment has been left literally on the Customer's doorstep in his absence. This situation must be avoided. The possibility of its being stolen or damaged under these circumstances is obvious, but what then is the legal position?

If the Contractor's Conditions of Sale state that responsibility for the Equipment rests with the Customer on delivery, the Contractor could be expected to argue very strongly that he had discharged his obligation by "delivering," regardless of the fact that no one may have been available to receive and sign for the delivery. It is obviously better to establish when Equipment and Software may be delivered so that proper arrangements can be made for their safe custody and protection. After all, it helps neither party if an essential item is stolen or damaged.

The clause also requires the Contractor to be responsible for providing all labor, materials, and plant required for the off-loading and placing in position of Equipment and Software. If lifting tackle is needed (or even four strong men) to off load the equipment and place it in position, it is unreasonable to expect the Customer to produce them specially; and even if he did, problems of liability would arise in the event of damage occurring during the unloading operations.

The question of liability in the event of theft or damage and the need to establish when property passes for insurance purposes means that there must be no ambiguity as to who is liable at any given time. Perhaps it is unfair to expect the Contractor to be liable for his equipment and tools when they are physically on the premises of the Customer, but damage is most likely to occur when the equipment is being installed by the Contractor's own employees, and Customers are unlikely to fail to satisfy the Contractor regarding the normal security arrangements on the premises. Most computer installations are subject to tight security, and unlike open sites, it is usually possible for the Customer to provide adequate, secure storage accommodation for the Contractor's use.

Subclause 8.2, which states that the authorization of the Contracting Officer is required for the Contractor to work on site, is complementary to subclause 4.2.1, which places the obligation on the Contracting Officer to grant access at all reasonable times.

CLAUSE 9. VARIATIONS

9.1 The Customer may at any time during the Contract require the Contractor to revise the Program of Works, including the Completion Date, and/or to undertake any reasonable alteration in, addition to, or omission from the Works or any part thereof (hereinafter referred to as a "Variation"). In the event of such a Variation being required, the Customer shall formally request the Contractor to state in writing the effect such Variation will have on the Works and what adjustment, if any, will be required to the Contract Price and to the Program of Works. The Contractor shall furnish such details within 14 days of receipt of the Customer's request or such other period as may be agreed. The Contractor shall not vary the Works in any respect unless instructed in writing to do so by the Customer.

9.2 A Variation under Subclause 9.1 shall not invalidate the Contract, but if such Variation involves an increase or decrease in the cost to the Contractor of carrying out the Works, an appropriate adjustment to the Contract Price shall be made. The Contractor shall satisfy the Customer as to the reasonableness of changes in the Program of Works and of the extra costs or savings resulting from Variations under this Clause.

EXPLANATORY NOTES

The clause gives the right to the Customer to make changes in the original contract in two areas—the Program of Works and the Works. These aspects will be dealt with separately.

Variations to the Program of Works

The date that the Contractor offers for the completion of the Contract and the subsequently agreed Program of Works is usually governed by the availability of either equipment coming off his production line or finished or semifinished bought-in components.

If the Customer wishes to advance the completion date, it usually means that the Contractor must give the Customer a higher priority for equipment coming off the line, or persuade his suppliers to give him priority. The extent to which this can be done will depend on the requirements of other customers. A Contractor will naturally try to accommodate a reasonable request, but the Customer must recognize that this is not a situation where working overtime or special

Model Form of Conditions of Contract

effort on the Contractor's part is likely to result in early delivery. The best that the Customer can normally hope for is an earlier delivery position at the expense of someone else. The situation is different where the Program of Works covers a total system and involves the installation of wiring and services and perhaps the writing of special software application packages. These are items where the provision of extra material resources, overtime work, or additional manpower can often enable programs to be advanced, but the Customer must be aware that such measures cost money and that he must pay for them. The question of how much money will be discussed later.

Where the Customer wants to delay completion, it is usually much easier for the Contractor to accommodate him. If the equipment is in high demand, then the Contractor is unlikely to experience difficulty in getting someone else to take an earlier delivery; if this is not so, or if the equipment has features which make it special to the Customer's requirements, then problems can arise. If the Contractor has suitable storage space, then any equipment coming off the line or being delivered by his suppliers can usually be safely stored until the later installation date. But even this can cost the Contractor money in the form of additional insurance, interest on outstanding money, double handling, and so forth, and once more the Customer will be liable. The problem is more acute when the Contractor has no suitable storage space, since he must then hire space or arrange with the Customer to store the equipment until it is time for installation. It is in these circumstances that problems can arise. Computer equipment is generally vulnerable to damage and pilferage, so what is the legal position if, by the time the revised installation date comes around, the equipment is not there or has been damaged? Unless otherwise agreed, the responsibility lies with the Contractor until the date when the Works are taken over by the Customer. In circumstances where this might prove to be an unacceptable risk to the Contractor, a mutual agreement must be reached between the parties.

Even in the case of a total system, it may prove difficult for the Contractor to redeploy his workforce and equipment onto other projects without incurring some costs. As in all other instances, if the Customer requires the alterations, he must expect to bear the cost.

Variations to the Works

In most cases, a Variation to the Works merely means adding a piece of equipment or deleting something, and the Contractor's ability to comply is obviously governed by the production situation. Most Contractors will happily agree to add to the list of equipment to be supplied under the Contract (although the effect on the Program of Works must not be overlooked), but are not so pleased to accept a deletion. Wherever it is practicable, the Customer has the right to require the Contractor to do both, but a word of warning is needed in case the Customer thinks that his right is unbounded.

It is obvious that a Contractor will do all in his power to sell additional equipment, but if he has ceased production of a particular piece of equipment, he is unlikely to be able to revert to its production, particularly if it is a one-time request. Theoretically he could produce one piece of equipment by special means, but this would undoubtedly cost a great deal of money which the Customer would not want to pay. The more usual situation is where the Contractor has replaced a piece of equipment by a later version, and although this may cause problems in a complete installation, it is likely to be the best that the Customer can expect at a reasonable price.

The deletion of equipment is always a practical proposition, but other considerations apply. If the Contractor has a full order book and if there are no special features on the Customer's equipment, he will often accept a deletion at no additional cost in order to maintain good customer relations. If the equipment is special or if his order book is bare and he thinks it unlikely that he can sell the item elsewhere, then it will obviously mean a loss for which he is entitled to be compensated. This is effectively a concellation charge, but unlike the standard cancellation charges often included in Contractor's Conditions of Sale, it is not based on a formula to be applied regardless of the circumstances of the cancellation. It gives the Contractor the right to recover the costs he has incurred by virtue of the deletion.

Variations required on total systems can cause severe problems to the Contractor and may even be impossible to implement. For example, if an on-line system under a Contract requires a certain response time based on a given throughput, then to request the response time to be halved against the same throughput (or the throughput to be doubled while maintaining the original response time) may be totally beyond the capacity of the equipment on which the Contract is based. Once again, Contractors will do everything possible to meet the Customer's requirements, but they must not be expected to achieve the impossible. In every case, the effect of Variations on program and price must not be overlooked.

Variations—Summary

To sum up, in requesting Variations to either the Program or the Works, the Customer must ensure that his requirements are within the scope of the Contract and that they are practicable and reasonable. He must also accept that any Variation can cause additional problems to the Contractor and that if these result in the Contractor's incurring additional costs, then the Customer is responsible for them.

Of the many problems that can arise over the instruction of Variations, the biggest of all, as far as the Customer is concerned, is the question of the agreement of additional costs.

It is hoped that the Customer has done some form of cost-benefit analysis before entering into a contract for the supply of computer equipment and that he will be conscious that any Variation is likely to upset the outcome. He should therefore ensure that he knows the effect on that analysis, before he orders a Variation to be made.

To know the effect of a proposed Variation, the Customer needs to obtain a written quotation from the Contractor, setting out the effect of the Variation in terms of both time and money. He can then decide from the effect these have on his cost-benefit analysis whether it is worthwhile to introduce the Variation.

In the operation of Variation Clauses in many types of Contract, Customers display a naive optimism about the cost of Variations, and often find when the bill is presented that the cost is much higher than expected. While informed buyers often have a great deal of information on which to base their cost estimates, only the Contractor knows the full effect, and it is common to find that areas of costs actually incurred—and therefore properly payable by the Customer—have not been envisaged by him.

Nonetheless, it is sometimes necessary to instruct a Variation before a quotation is received, and the clause requires the Contractor to satisfy the Customer as to the reasonableness of the proposed changes to the Program of Works and the extra costs or savings resulting from the Variation. Once more, the Customer must not be unreasonable in his demands for cost justification. (For example, published list prices are usually regarded as ample justification, and it would be unreasonable to ask for details of production costs.) Costs arising from the provision of additional material resources and labor hours are usually based on estimated times and generally recognizable rates and costs, and a breakdown of the sum of additional costs usually enables agreement to be reached fairly quickly.

As in all forms of contracting, a reasonable attitude toward the recognition of the other party's difficulties in either providing cost details or justifying acceptance will help bring negotiations to a satisfactory conclusion.

CLAUSE 10. EXTENSION OF TIME FOR COMPLETION

If, after the date of the award of the Contract, the Contractor shall have been delayed or impeded by any act or omission of the Customer or any circumstances beyond the reasonable control of the Contractor—and provided that the Contractor shall without delay have notified the Customer in writing of such delay or impedance—the Contracting Officer shall grant the Contractor from time to time in writing such extension as may be reasonable, and the Completion Date shall be amended accordingly.

EXPLANATORY NOTES

The rationale behind this clause is simple: If the actions of the Customer or circumstances beyond the Contractor's reasonable control prevent him from completing the Contract on time, then he is entitled to an extension of time for completion. He may also be entitled to additional costs resulting from the Customer's default, but it must be borne in mind that an extension of time does not always result in additional costs. The application of this clause is also simple, but some explanations and warnings need to be offered.

As stated above, there are two reasons why a Contractor may be entitled to an extension of time. The first is where the Customer is in default. Since this is a matter of fact, there is usually little difficulty in establishing that an extension should be granted. For example, if the Customer's premises are not ready to receive the equipment on the date scheduled, and if a delay in completion occurs, there is no doubt that the Customer is in default. The main requirement then is for the Contractor to notify the Customer in writing immediately when he is aware of the delay or impedance and, if possible, to inform him of the likely consequences.

The second set of circumstances that can justify an extension of time—namely, circumstances outside the Contractor's reasonable control—can cause much more difficulty. The problem is to determine just what is outside the Contractor's reasonable control. If there is a national strike or his factory is hit by secondary strikes or boycotts then there is little he can do to prevent delays. But what is the position where a small local stoppage is caused by the intransigence of management? Fortunately stoppages that fall into this second category are comparatively rare (or it may be that they are difficult to prove), and labor disputes generally qualify for an extension of time.

Difficulties occur more often when a Contractor claims that shortages of materials, or failures on the part of his suppliers or Subcontractors, have caused delays. Such failures would not normally constitute reasons for an extension of time. The performance of the Contractor's suppliers and Subcontractors is entirely his responsibility, and it is for him to ensure that they are reliable before he appoints them. After all, the Contractor is the expert in all matters relating to the supply of his equipment. He must recognize that this imposes responsibilities upon him which he cannot avoid.

There is, then, the question of the responsibility for additional costs arising in those instances where an extension of time is granted. If the Customer is in default, then any unavoidable additional costs can be recovered by the Contractor, but he is required by law to take all reasonable steps to mitigate the effect of the Customer's default and to minimize such costs, and he will be required to demonstrate the extent of the additional costs incurred. Where an extension is granted because of "circumstances beyond the reasonable control of the Contractor," this becomes a misfortune where both sides suffer and where it would be unreasonable to expect either side to bear all the costs. In these circumstances, the usual solution is that, in granting an extension of time, the Contractor is relieved of all his obligations to complete the project by the original completion date, but no additional costs are recoverable from the Customer.

One further piece of advice on the operation of this clause may be helpful: Deal with the situations when they arise. So many contracts end up in complicated disputes because the parties did not deal promptly with situations that required extensions of time. Memories fade and records are seldom perfect, so that any retrospective settlement becomes more and more difficult as time goes by.

CLAUSE 11. DELAYS
11.1 *Delays by the Contractor.*
If the Contractor fails to complete the Works by the Completion Date or such revised date as may be agreed or granted in accordance with Clauses 9 and 10, and if, as a result, the Customer shall have suffered a loss, the Customer shall have the right to deduct from the Contract Price the percentage stated in the Appendix to these Conditions of the Contract Price of the Works or of such portions of the Works as cannot in consequence of said failure be put to the use intended for each week between the Completion Date or revised Completion Date and the actual Acceptance Date. The amount so deducted, however, shall not in any case exceed the maximum percentage stated in the Appendix of the Contract Price of the Works or of such portion or portions of the Works, and such deduction shall be in full satisfaction of the Contractor's liability for the said failure.

11.2 *Time the Essence of the Contract.*
In the event that the Contract states that time is the essence of the Contract, then Subclause 11.1 shall not apply and, if the Contractor fails to complete the Works by the Completion Date or any agreed revised date, the Contract will be voidable at the option of the Customer. Whether or not that option is exercised, the Customer shall have the right to recover from the Contractor all costs resulting from such failure.

11.3 *Delays by the Customer.*
All additional expenses reasonably incurred by the Contractor by reason of his being prevented from or delayed in proceeding with the Works by the Customer, by some other contractor employed by the Customer, or by reason of suspension of the Works by the Customer (otherwise than in consequence of some default on the part of the Contractor), shall be reimbursed to the Contractor by the Customer, provided that no claim shall be made under this Clause unless the Contractor has, within 14 days after the event leading to the claim, given notice to the Customer in writing of his intention to make such a claim.

EXPLANATORY NOTES

"Delays by the Contractor" (Clause 11.1)

The general position in British law is that if a Contractor fails to complete his obligations under a Contract by the agreed completion date, and the Customer thereby suffers a loss, then the Customer is entitled to claim damages at large for the losses he has suffered by virtue of the Contractor's default. What this means in practice is that a Customer has to initiate litigation to claim his costs (an expensive and lengthy undertaking) and the Contractor has no way of knowing what claims he may face in the event that he delays completion.

All contracting is a risky business and in pricing his products and services, the Contractor seeks, among other things, to price the resources he has to commit and the risks associated with his obligations under the Contract. The resources at his disposal can usually be fairly accurately priced, but all risks need to be evaluated and covered by contingencies, which may or may not be needed. The Contractor is, therefore, faced with a dilemma. If he thinks the risk associated with a Contract is high, he would like to include a contingency large enough to buffer him against the risk, but competition usually precludes such a provision. If the risks are completely unknown (for example, where losses likely to be suffered by the Customer in the event of delay are completely unquantified), then how can he price for this risk with any degree of accuracy?

In practice, what happens is that Contractors will not usually give any firm commitment on delivery or Contract completion, using terms in their Conditions of Sale such as "delivery subject to availability" or "no undertaking can be given regarding delivery, but the Contractor will use his best efforts." This is reasonable when risks cannot be evaluated, but it leaves the Customer in a very difficult position. The Customer buys a computer in the expectation that its use will bring him benefits, and these will have been evaluated by a cost-benefit analysis based on the availability of the equipment for his use. The nonreceipt of equipment on time will obviously alter those calculations, and the absence of guarantees of delivery means that he can have no real confidence that any evaluation will be effective.

The solution to this impasse is a "Liquidated Damages"-type clause in which the Customer gives a pre-estimate of what his losses will be in the event of delayed delivery and the Contractor can evaluate the risk of having to meet such a claim, based on his knowledge of current supply problems and of what delivery promises have meant in the past. This enables a Contractor to give a guarantee of delivery and completion, and the Customer to make his cost-benefit calculations and to plan his future operations with some confidence.

This clause, therefore, requires the Customer to make a pre-estimate of what his losses will be in the event of a delay and to express them in the form of a percentage of the Contract Price. When issuing invitations to bid, the Customer needs to state the percentage of the Contract Price that he will deduct for each week of delay and the maximum percentage that can be deducted. A genuine pre-estimate is extremely difficult to make. The usual provision is something on the basis of 1 per cent per week up to a maximum of 10 per cent. Whatever the percentage included, the Customer must ensure that it is not penal; penal damages can be challenged and will not be upheld in the courts. The point to remember is that the higher the percentages, the more risk the Contractor carries and the more he will feel entitled to include high contingencies in his quoted price.

In the event of failure to complete the project on time, the Customer is entitled to deduct the agreed proportion of the Contract Price without recourse to litigation, provided that he has suffered a loss.

"Time the Essence of the Contract" (Clause 11.2)

Contracts where "time is of the essence" are extremely rare, and this subclause (which is an alternative to Clause 11.1) will usually be deleted in computer contracts. The requirement envisaged by this clause is at the opposite end of the spectrum from the usual situation where the Contractor will give no guarantees of delivery or completion.

What the clause means is that if completion is not made by the agreed Completion Date, then the Customer has the right to cancel the Contract and charge the Contractor any costs that have been incurred. This obviously becomes a very high risk Contract as far as the Contractor is concerned, and in the event that the is prepared to accept such a Contract, he would have to be very sure of achieving the Completion Date or he would almost certainly include a very high contingency sum in his price. Conversely, if the Customer feels that a Completion Date is so important that he requires time to be of the essence, then he must expect to pay heavily.

"Delays by the Customer" (Clause 11.3)

This is an enabling clause, and its operation needs to be in accordance with Clause 10 (Extension of Time for Completion). The only additional point to make is that there is a time limit within which the Contractor must advise the Customer that a situation has occurred which may give rise to a claim. The Customer would not expect a detailed evaluation of the claim at this time, but would require notice of the circumstances so that a decision could be made jointly concerning the actions to be taken to alleviate them. It is also a good disciplinary action in that it warns both sides that a potentially difficult situation has arisen and should dispel the complacency that often exists in these situations. When circumstances occur that give rise to delay, they seldom cure themselves; remedial action is necessary if trouble is to be averted.

CLAUSE 12. FACTORY TESTS

12.1 Subject to giving the Contractor reasonable notice, the Customer shall be entitled at all reasonable times during manufacture to inspect, examine, and test at the Contractor's facilities the materials, workmanship, and performance of all the Equipment and Software to be supplied under the Contract. If part of the said Equipment and Software is being manufactured elsewhere, the Contractor shall obtain for the Customer permission to inspect, examine, and test it as if it were being manufactured at the Contractor's facilities. Such inspection, examination, or testing shall not release the Contractor from any of his obligations under the Contract.

12.2 The Contractor shall give the Customer 14 days' written notice of the date and the place at which any Equipment or Software that is subject to Factory Tests will be ready for testing. If the Customer shall decline or fail to attend at the place so named and on the date which the Contractor has stated in his notice, the Contractor may proceed with the Factory Tests (which shall be deemed to have been made in the Customer's presence) and shall forward to the Customer daily certified copies of the test readings. The Customer shall give the Contractor notice in writing of his intention to attend the Factory Tests.

12.3 Where the Contract provides for Factory Tests, the Contractor shall, except where otherwise specified, include in the Contract Price for such assistance, labor, materials, electricity, fuel, stores, apparatus, and instruments as may be requisite and may reasonably be required to carry out the Factory Tests efficiently.

12.4 If and when the Equipment and Software have passed the Factory Tests, the Customer shall notify the Contractor in writing to that effect.

12.5 If, after inspecting, examining, or testing any Equipment and Software, the Equipment and Software or any part thereof is defective or is not in accordance with the Contract, the Customer may reject the said Equipment and Software or any part thereof within 14 days of the date of such inspection, examination, or testing notice by notifying the Contractor in writing of such rejection, stating therein the grounds upon which the rejection is based.

12.6 If any Equipment or Software fails to pass the Factory Tests or is rejected under Subclause 12.5, such Equipment or Software shall be tested again within a reasonable time upon the same terms and conditions, but all reasonable expenses to which the Customer may be put by the repetition of the tests shall be reimbursed to the Customer by the Contractor.

EXPLANATORY NOTES

This clause is unlikely to be used by any buyer who does not have a substantial technical backup facility and, even then, probably only on special-purpose equipment or custom-built configurations. The computer user who is buying a standard model should not expect to be able to inspect the Contractor's works during manufacture since, apart from the obvious problems, the particular materials and components associated with his equipment are unlikely ever to be identified.

The other reason why the buyer of a standard model would be unlikely to require factory tests is that such equipment is usually well specified in the manufacturer's literature, and specific factory tests will cost money and are unlikely to serve any useful purpose. If factory tests are not required, the clause should be deleted.

If, however, factory tests are required, then full details of what these will entail should be included in the invitation to bid, so as to enable the bidder to include the cost of them in his bid price.

CLAUSE 13. ACCEPTANCE TESTS

13.1 The Contractor shall give to the Customer in writing seven days' prior notice—or such shorter notice as may be agreed—of the date when he will be ready to commence the Acceptance Tests. Unless otherwise agreed, the tests shall take place on the said date(s) or on such later date(s) as the Customer shall notify the Contractor about in writing.

13.2 If the Customer fails to attend on the appointed date(s) for the Acceptance Tests, the Contractor shall be entitled to proceed in his absence, and the said tests shall be deemed to have been made in the presence of the Customer. Copies of all documents produced as a result of the tests shall be made available to the Customer.

13.3 If, in the opinion of the Customer, the Acceptance Tests are being unreasonably delayed, he may give written notice to the Contractor, requiring him to make the said tests within seven days from receipt of the said notice. The Contractor shall make the said tests on such date(s) within the said seven days as the Contractor may fix and of which he shall give reasonable notice to the Customer. If the Contractor fails to make such tests within the specified time, the Customer may himself proceed to make said tests. All Acceptance Tests so made by the Customer shall be at the risk and expense of the Contractor, unless the Contractor shall establish that said tests were not being delayed, in which case such tests so made shall be at the risk and expense of the Customer.

13.4 If the Equipment and Software or any portion thereof fails to pass the Acceptance Tests, repeat tests shall be carried out within a reasonable time upon the same terms and conditions but at the sole expense of the Contractor. In the event that the repeat tests show that the Equipment and Software are not in accordance with the Contract, then the Customer shall have the right to:

(i) Require the Contractor to supply, free of charge, such additional or replacement Equipment and Software as may be necessary to enable the Equipment and Software to pass the Acceptance Tests; *or*

(ii) Accept and retain such of the Equipment and Software as he may consider expedient at such reduced price as may be agreed between the Customer and the Contractor; *or*

(iii) Reject the Equipment and Software where it is not in accordance with the Contract.

EXPLANATORY NOTES

Most computer manufacturers have a standard series of tests that they carry out on equipment after it has been installed in a Customer's premises, and it is for the Customer to ensure that the Contractor's proposals in this respect are satisfactory before the Contract is placed. The cost of standard tests is

Model Form of Conditions of Contract

almost invariably included in list prices, but if additional tests are required, then the buyer must specify his requirements in detail so that the bidder can include any additional cost in his offer.

The clause starts from the premise that the Contract contains agreement on the tests to be carried out. The first part of the clause (Clause 13.1) requires the Contractor to give the Customer seven days' notice of the date on which he will be ready to commence the Acceptance Tests. Such notice, or a shorter period if agreed to by both parties, is necessary to enable the Customer to arrange for his technical specialist to be available when the tests are carried out. The situation must be avoided where the Contractor arrives on site without prior warning and insists on carrying out the Acceptance Tests regardless of whether or not this is acceptable to the Customer.

If the Customer is unable to make the arrangements he considers necessary for witnessing the tests on the date proposed by the Contractor, he may notify the Contractor in writing of a date that will be suitable. In most cases a mutually acceptable date will be achieved without any difficulty, but the Customer must recognize that if he delays the tests to the extent that it prevents achievement of the Completion Date, then he may be faced with a request for an extension of time and a claim for additional costs.

If, after making arrangements for the tests, the Customer finds that his representative cannot attend, then the Contractor is entitled to go ahead with the tests (Clause 13.2), but must make all test results available to the Customer.

Clause 13.3 gives the Customer the right to require the Contractor to carry out the Acceptance Tests if he thinks that the tests are being unreasonably delayed. The key to the operation of this clause is the question of what constitutes unreasonable delay. Bearing in mind the remedies that the Customer has under Clause 11 (Delays) and the fact that the

Contractor has only limited resources, then if he decides that another customer should have priority, the Customer may go ahead and carry out the tests himself. Needless to say, this is an extreme measure and carries with it the risk that if the Equipment fails to pass its test, the Contractor will say that either the tests have not been carried out correctly or the Equipment has been damaged by the Customer in carrying out the tests. In either case, since the original default is with the Contractor, all risks and expenses will be for his account.

The situation where, despite repeat tests, the Equipment fails the Acceptance Tests is covered in Clause 13.4. This provides for three possible solutions:

1. *Where the Equipment provided under the contract is demonstrably unsatisfactory, but where it is in the Contractor's power to remedy the situation.* If an individual piece of standard equipment fails to meet its specified performance, then the fault is likely to be with the materials and workmanship rather than with a deficiency in design. Replacement will usually ensure satisfactory performance. However, the situation is more difficult where the specification is based on the performance of the whole configuration. In this case, the individual pieces of equipment may meet all the manufacturer's specifications, but the design of the configuration may be inadequate. In such a case, where the Contractor has agreed that his configuration will meet the Customer's performance on workload requirements, then it is his responsibility to supply, free of charge, any additional items necessary to enable performance to be achieved.

2. *Where the Equipment is unsatisfactory, but the Customer is prepared to accept a lower performance than the specified one.* If the Contractor fails to supply Equipment to the standard agreed in the Contract, it is open to the Customer to accept the Equipment, recognizing that he will obtain a lower than specified performance level. He will, of

course, receive a lower rate of return on his investment and, in recognition of this, the price of the unsatisfactory items should be reduced by agreement between the parties.

3. *Where the Equipment is unsatisfactory and the Customer is not prepared to accept a lower performance than the specified one and thus rejects the Equipment.* This is the worst situation of all, because the Contractor is in breach of contract and is liable to the Customer for all the legal remedies that go with such a breach—and the Customer does not get his equipment. Clearly, this is a situation to be avoided by both parties if at all possible.

CLAUSE 14. ACCEPTANCE CERTIFICATE

14.1 As soon as the Works have been completed in accordance with the Contract and have passed the Acceptance Tests, the Contracting Officer shall issue an Acceptance Certificate which will state the Acceptance Date and any outstanding defects in the Works.

14.2 If by agreement between the Customer and the Contractor any part of the Works shall be satisfactorily completed in advance of the remainder, the Contracting Officer may issue an Acceptance Certificate in respect of that part.

EXPLANATORY NOTES

The Acceptance Certificate is a most important document, because it signifies acceptance by the Customer that the Works have passed into his hands and that responsibility for safekeeping is now with him. This obviously covers responsibilities for damage and insurance of the property. It also normally means that the Customer can put the Works into operational use.

It will be noted (Clause 14.1) that the Works can be accepted even if they have some defects (which must be listed on the Acceptance Certificate). The reason for this is that the Customer will undoubtedly be anxious to put the Equipment to operational use, and if the defects are not serious enough to prevent this, then the sensible solution is to take the Equipment over but to require the Contractor to remedy the defects as soon as possible. Normally the Customer will retain a sum of money to cover defect rectification and will make payment only when the defects are remedied.

The other part of the clause (14.2) enables the Customer to accept parts of the Works in advance of full completion. This may be satisfactory to both parties—to the Contractor, because responsibility then passes to the Customer, and payment for that part of the Works may be obtained; and to the Customer, who can start using that part of the Works.

CLAUSE 15. PATENTS, DESIGNS, AND COPYRIGHT

15.1 The Contractor shall fully indemnify the Customer against all actions, claims, demands, proceedings, damages, costs, charges, and expenses arising from or incurred by reason of any infringement or alleged infringement of Patents, Designs, or Copyright by the use or possession of the Equipment and Software supplied by the Contractor under the Contract, subject to the following conditions:

(i) The Customer shall promptly notify the Contractor in writing of any alleged infringement of which he has notice.

(ii) The Customer must make no admissions without the Contractor's consent.

(iii) The Customer, at the Contractor's request and expense, shall allow the Contractor to conduct and/or settle all negotiations and litigation and give the Contractor all reasonable assistance. The costs incurred or recovered in such negotiations or litigation shall be for the Contractor's account.

15.2 If at any time any allegation of infringement of Patents, Designs, or Copyright is made with respect to the Equipment and Software or in the Contractor's reasonable opinion is likely to be made, the Contractor may at his own expense modify or replace the Equipment and Software without detracting from overall performance. The Contractor must make good to the Customer any loss of use during modification or replacement, so as to avoid the infringement. The provisions of Clause 9 shall then take effect as if the Customer had required a Variation, save that the Contractor shall not be entitled to request any increase to the Contract Price.

EXPLANATORY NOTES

This clause makes it clear that any infringement of Patents, Designs, or Copyright in the Equipment or Software is the Contractor's responsibility—and this must be so, for both the design of the Equipment and the writing of the Software are normally done by the Contractor. The rest of the clause is purely the mechanism for dealing with a situation where there is an alleged infringement or where the Contractor recognizes his infringement and seeks to remedy the situation.

In the rare event of a Customer's design being included in some part of the Works, or where he requires the Contractor to include in the Equipment an item or feature of his own, then it is for the Contractor to reserve his position before the Contract is placed.

All computer manufacturers and software houses are very aware of the dangers of infringement and are likely to have a great deal of expertise available in this field, so any problems are as a matter of common sense best left to them.

CLAUSE 16. STANDARD OF PERFORMANCE
The Contractor shall ensure that the Equipment and Software maintain the Standard of Performance specified in the Contract and demonstrated in the Acceptance Tests for *either*

(i) The period of the maintenance Contract, if the Equipment and/or Software are to maintained by the Contractor;
(ii) The Warranty Period, if the Equipment and/or Software are not to be maintained by the Contractor.

If the Customer can demonstrate that the Standard of Performance specified in the Contract has not been maintained, and it is the fault of the Contractor, then, notwithstanding prior acceptance of the Equipment and Software in accordance with Clauses 13 and 14, the Contractor shall forthwith, at his own expense, provide to the Customer such replacement or additional items of Equipment and Software as may be necessary to achieve the Standard of Performance specified in the Contract.

EXPLANATORY NOTES

This short clause has been the subject of as much discussion as any other clause in the Model Conditions, and the following is an outline of the problems and an explanation of the rationale behind what was eventually included.

The reason for the inclusion of the clause is that a customer wants to be sure that the performance specified in the Contract and demonstrated in the Acceptance Tests be maintained. The obligation on the Contractor is to ensure that there is no degradation in the Standard of Performance for as long as he continues to be responsible for the ongoing maintenance of the Works. If the Contractor is not responsible for maintenance, then the normal commercial requirement for satisfactory performance during a warranty period (in the case of these Conditions, 12 months) should apply.

The argument against the inclusion of such a clause is that after the Acceptance Tests, which demonstrate that the Equipment and Software are satisfactory at that time, the customer commences operational use, using his own operators and very often his own Software application packages. In these circumstances, the Contractor can argue that any deterioration in performance is probably a result of one of these two factors, since the performance of electronic equipment does not in itself suffer progressive deterioration.

There is clearly truth in this argument, and because the Equipment is the property of—and is operated by—the Customer, it is only fair that the onus should be on him to demonstrate that any deterioration in the Standard of Performance is the fault of the Contractor. This demonstration is likely to be difficult: If what the Customer has bought under the Contract is a piece of Equipment which is now included in a larger configuration, then how can he be sure that a lower Standard of Performance is a result of the deterioration of that piece of Equipment and not of the interaction of other units? If he adds an attachment or removes part of the Equipment, how will this affect performance?

Difficulties are even more apparent where Software is concerned. An inefficient application package will undoubtedly affect throughput and response times, and any Customer updates to Software supplied under the Contract can obviously have an effect on Standards of Performance. In addition to this, the Equipment, once taken over by the Customer, might be interfered with either by the Customer or by an unauthorized third party, or might even be operated inefficiently, and the Contractor has no control over any of these matters.

To summarize, the Customer must demonstrate that deterioration in performance is the fault of the Contractor if remedies are to apply, but demonstrating that is likely to be very difficult indeed. One ray of hope in this area seems to be that technical developments and diagnostic aids are constantly improving. These, coupled with special developments in the Software field, such as synthetic benchmark packages which can simulate the criteria that existed at the time of acceptance testing, should aid the Customer in the future.

The ability of the Customer to demonstrate performance standards will undoubtedly follow in due course; the establishment of the principle that the Contractor should be responsible for degradation of performance is the important factor.

CLAUSE 17. ASSIGNMENT AND SUBLETTING

17.1 The Contractor shall not assign, pledge, or transfer the Contract or any of the rights or obligations therein without the prior written consent of the Customer.

17.2 The Contractor shall not, without the written consent of the Customer (which shall not be unreasonably withheld), sublet the Contract or any part thereof or make any Subcontract with any person or persons for the execution of any party of the Works, but the restriction contained in this Clause shall not apply to the supply of materials or minor details nor to any part of the Works for which a Subcontractor is named in the Contract. Any such consent shall not relieve the Contractor from any of his obligations under the Contract.

EXPLANATORY NOTES

The rationale for this clause is that, having made a Contract with a particular firm, the Customer does not then want to find himself dealing with someone else, either for payments and administration or for performance of the Contract. However, provided that arrangements are satisfactory to the Customer, he can give his consent, rights and/or obligations can be transferred, and Subcontractors can take over such performance aspects as are agreed upon.

Note that the clause does not prohibit the Contractor from buying components, and any restrictions in this area would be unrealistic. It does, however, ensure that the final responsibility for performance is with the Contractor.

CLAUSE 18. INDEMNITY AND INSURANCE

18.1 The Contractor shall indemnify and keep indemnified the Customer against injury (including death) to any persons or loss of or damage to any property—including the Equipment and Software—which may arise out of the act, default, or negligence of the Contractor, Subcontractor, and their employees or agent, as well as against all claims, demands, proceedings, damages, costs, charges, and expenses whatsoever in respect thereof or in relation thereto, provided that the Contractor shall not be liable for the Customer nor be required to indemnify him against any compensation or damages for or with respect to injuries, or damage to persons or property, to the extent that such injuries or damage result wholly from any act, default, or negligence on the part of the Customer, his employees, or contractors (who are not the Contractor or employed by the Contractor).

18.2 The Customer shall indemnify and keep indemnified the Contractor for the duration of the Contract against injury (including death) to any persons or loss of or damage to any property (including the Equipment and Software) which may arise out of the act, default, or negligence of the Customer or any contractor employed by the Customer (other than the Contractor) and against all claims, demands, proceedings, damages, costs, charges, and expenses whatsoever in respect thereof or in relation thereto.

18.3 Without thereby limiting his responsibilities under Subclause 18.1, the Contractor shall insure with a reputable insurance company against all loss of and damage to property and injury to persons (including death) arising out of or in consequence of the Contractor's obligations under the Contract and against all actions, claims, demands, costs, and expenses in respect thereof, save only as is set out in the exceptions in Subclauses 18.4 and 18.5.

18.4 Except with respect to injury (including death) to any person other than the Customer or loss of or damage to any property not belonging to the Customer, the liability of the Contractor to the Customer under Subclause 18.1 in respect of any one act or default shall not exceed the sum stated in the Appendix to these conditions.

18.5 The Contractor shall not be liable to the Customer for loss of use, profit, or contracts suffered by the Customer and arising out of such injury or damage.

EXPLANATORY NOTES

As the heading of this clause indicates, it covers two aspects of liability between the parties, but it also defines where those liabilities lie. Before dealing with the detail, however, it is necessary to make sure there is no ambiguity in the meaning of the two terms.

To indemnify someone is to give him security against loss, damage, or penalty and to reimburse him for expenditure incurred—in other words, it is the acceptance of responsibility for the incident involved. This is fine as far as it goes, but if the person giving the indemnity does not have the means to give reimbursement, then the indemnity is worthless and some mechanism is required to ensure that those responsibilities can be met. This is where the requirement for insurance (the acceptance of risk by many against the misfortunes of the few) applies, and it is common knowledge that, in return for payment of a premium, insurance companies will undertake to cover risks on behalf of the person responsible under the Contract.

Subclause 18.1

This subclause puts the responsibility on the Contractor for any accident, damage, or claims arising on the Contract, excepting only those cases where the accident, damage, or claim arises out of the default of the Customer or of anyone engaged by him, either as employees, agents, or other contractors. This type of clause is fairly common in contracts, and most contractors carry "all-risks" insurances covering all claims against them with respect to their normal contracting activities. The clause effectively means that the Contractor accepts the risks associated with the normal business in which he is engaged—some of which are statutory requirements, in any case.

Subclause 18.2

This fills the gap left by the exception in Subclause 18.1 and says that the Customer must bear responsibility for the consequences of his "act, default, or negligence." In other words, he accepts responsibility for those accidents, damages, or claims caused by himself, his employees or agents, or other contractors employed by him.

Subclause 18.3

The indemnities required under the previous subclauses are worthless if the money is not available to meet consequent claims, and this subclause requires the Contractor to take out an insurance policy against his risk. The insurance for the Works and for the Customer's property should ideally be in the joint names of the Contractor and Customer so that any recompense will go to the party that has suffered damage. For example, if the Contractor damages the Customer's property, it is the Contractor's liability, but the insurance payment would be made direct to the Customer, so that he can fix the damage.

Subclause 18.4

Except for liability with respect to injury or death, for which the Contractor has a statutory liability, the Customer can limit the Contractor's liability under subclause 18.1 to the figure named in the Appendix.

It is, therefore, up to the Customer to insert the limit figure in the Appendix, and in the absence of any amount having been inserted, there is no limitation. This may appear to be the best course of action for the Customer—but it is not.

In the long run, the cost of insurance is passed on to the Customer in the overheads included in the Contractor's selling price, and any special insurance would be charged extra. If no limit is specified, then the Contractor may decide to insure at a very high level, in which case the Customer will be paying more than necessary, or he may quote on the basis of the figure he considers to be adequate, which, in practice, may be lower than required.

Where insurance is concerned, the best advice is to be realistic.

Subclause 18.5

This subclause limits the liability of the Contractor under subclause 18.1 by excluding any Customer's claims for loss of use of the damaged property or any profit that might have been made by him had the damage not occurred.

CLAUSE 19. TERMS OF PAYMENT

19.1 The Contractor shall be entitled to claim payment of the percentage payments detailed in the Appendix to these Conditions of the Contract Price of the Works or any part thereof on the issue of an Acceptance Certificate under Clause 14. The remaining percentage of the Contract Price shall become due on completion by the Contractor of his obligations under Clause 23 (Warranty Period).

19.2 If at any time at which any payment is supposed to be made under Subclause 19.1 there shall be any defect due to the fault of the Contractor in or affecting any portion of the Works in respect to which such payment is claimed, the Customer shall have the right to retain the whole of such payment (provided that in the event such defect is of a minor character and not such as to affect the use of the Works or the said portion thereof for the purpose intended without serious risk, the Customer shall not retain a greater sum than represents the cost of making good said defect). Any sum retained by the Customer under this Clause shall be paid to the Contractor when said defect is made good.

19.3 Applications for payment or invoices with respect to all charges and payments due under the Contract shall be rendered in accordance with the procedures detailed in the Contract. Payment shall be due within 30 days of receipt by the Customer of a correct application for payment, or invoice, or as otherwise specified in the Contract.

19.4 The Customer reserves the right to withhold payment against any invoice which is not submitted in accordance with the Contract or which covers or purports to relate to Equipment, Software, or services which have not been provided in accordance with the Contract and shall forthwith notify the Contractor accordingly in writing.

19.5 If the payment of any sum due under the Contract shall be delayed by the Customer other than in accordance with Subclauses 19.2 and 19.4, the Contractor shall be entitled to charge interest at the rate of 1 percent per annum over the current prime rate on the amount of the delayed payment for the period of the delay.

EXPLANATORY NOTES

Payment clauses are inevitably mechanistic and, if either the Customer or the Contractor has special payment requirements, these should be made clear at the stage of invitation or offer. Again, the effect of any alterations to standard clauses needs to be understood.

The first problem that the Customer encounters if a Contractor quotes different payment terms is the achievement of a common basis for the evaluation of offers. This is obviously not a serious problem and can be resolved by a relatively simple arithmetical calculation, but payment with order (or a large percentage) or payment on delivery (that is, before the Equipment has been installed or tested on site) immediately puts the Customer at risk. If everything goes well, the risk may turn out to be nonexistent, but it is when things go wrong and the Contractor has no monetary incentive to put them right that the Customer would have reason to regret early payment. The situation if a Contractor goes into liquidation is even more precarious from the Customer's point of view, for unless the Equipment paid for has been marked as the property of the Customer, he has little chance of getting any real return—in either money or equipment.

Subclause 19.1

The retention of monies after the Works have been accepted is something to which many Contractors object, and in many cases payment of 100 percent of the Contract Price on acceptance is warranted. If what the Customer is buying is a standard piece of well-tried and trusted equipment, and if good long-term relationships have been established with the Contractor, then retention of a percentage of the Contract Price is not recommended. In this case, 100 percent is the figure to be inserted in the appropriate space in the Appendix to the Conditions.

If, on the other hand, the Customer considers it prudent to retain a sum of money to ensure that the Contractor carries out his obligations during the Warranty Period (see Clause 23), then a lower percentage figure should be inserted. As usual, reason should prevail, and the retention percentage should be kept as small as possible. Cash flow is always a problem and, if the Contractor has to finance a sum for a period of 12 months, then he is going to charge for it. The sum retained should never be greater than is estimated to be sufficient to ensure that the Contractor will carry out his obligations during that period.

Subclause 19.2

The Customer's rights to retain payment, or part payment, in the event that defects become apparent by the time payments are due is a sensible and equitable provision, provided that payment of any sum retained is made as soon as the defect has been rectified.

Subclause 19.3
This is purely mechanistic, and if 30 days is too long (or too short) a period, then this can be altered to suit the parties. Remember, though, that if the period for payment is protracted, the Contractor is entitled to include extra finance charges in his price.

Subclause 19.4
The Customer is clearly entitled to withhold payment for anything not in accordance with the Contract, but the important part of this clause is that he must then write to the Contractor without delay and tell him why he is withholding payment. If the Contractor makes a mistake in invoicing, he must correct it, but he must not be penalized by causing rightful payment to be withheld for longer than necessary.

Subclause 19.5
The Contractor's entitlement to payment in accordance with the Contract is recognized in this Clause, and the disincentive to the Customer to delay payment is that he is required to pay interest on delayed payments if they are delayed through no fault of the Contractor.

CLAUSE 20. VARIATIONS IN COSTS
if, by reason of any rise or fall in the cost of materials, labor, or transport (above or below such costs ruling at the date of bid), the cost to the Contractor of performing his obligations under the Contract shall be increased or reduced, the amount of such increase or reduction shall be added to or deducted from the Contract Price as the case may be, provided that no account shall be taken of any amount by which any cost

incurred by the Contractor has been increased by the default or negligence of the Contractor. The amount of such increase or reduction shall be calculated in accordance with the formula detailed in the Contract.

EXPLANATORY NOTES

Most experienced buyers advise that the worst possible type of Contract to be forced into is the one where on price is specified (orders placed on a "price to be advised" basis) or where a price is stated but the Conditions of Sale stipulate that the price will be that ruling at date of delivery. In neither case does he know what his commitment is, and any cost-benefit analyses he has done could be totally invalidated. However, if a Contractor is required to price for work which will not be performed until a considerable time after his quotation, it might be impracticable for him to quot a fixed price, particularly in times of high inflation. Alternatively, he will include a contingency which may either under- or overrecover any actual increased costs incurred—a risk in either event.

A Variations in Cost Clause—or Cost Price Adjustment (CPA) Clause, as it is sometimes known—is the usual contractual answer to the problem. The theoretical base for the clause is that, if prices vary in the period between quotation and performance of the Contract, then rather than either party's taking a risk by the inclusion in the price of a contingency sum that is either inadequate or overstated, the Contract is placed on prices prevailing at the time of the quotation, and any increases or decreases in costs which are outside the control of the Contractor (for example, cost-of-living increases) are reimbursed.

This reimbursement is sometimes done on an "actual" basis, where the Contract Price is broken down into identifiable components and documentation is produced by the

Model Form of Conditions of Contract

Contractor to verify the increased costs he has paid. This is a time-consuming administrative chore and is open to many abuses. To avoid this unsatisfactory situation, many Variations in Cost Clauses are based on formulas on which the increases in costs are calculated, and since the clause in these Conditions is so based, it is this method that will be explained here.

The first thing to appreciate about a formula is that it is a "broad brush" and is not intended to reimburse exactly the additional costs on individual Contracts. It should, however, be reasonably accurate over a span of Contracts and time.

What a formula is intended to do is to divide Contract costs into broad identifiable cost headings, such as labor, materials, transport, overheads, and profit, and then apply an accepted yardstick to each. The obvious yardsticks are government statistics on movements in prices, which are published by the U.S. Department of Commerce, but price movement indexes published by any reputable independent agencies are usually acceptable, too.

As an example of a formula, let us assume a simple breakdown of costs: 40 percent labor, 40 percent material, 20 percent overheads and profit. Assume that transport is not a significant factor, and that increases in the other components will compensate for increased transport cost. In this case, the formula could be:

$$A = \left[40 \times \left\{ \frac{L_2 - L_1}{L_1} \right\} + 40 \times \left\{ \frac{M_2 - M_1}{M_1} \right\} + 20 \times \left\{ \frac{O_2 - O_1}{O_1} \right\} \right] \times 100$$

Where A = percentage adjustment of contract price
L_1 = labor index at price base date
L_2 = labor index at time of claim

M_1 = materials index at price base date
M_2 = materials index at time of claim
O_1 = overheads index at price base date
O_2 = overheads index at time of claim

This formula is simple and capable of infinite refinement; in fact, many trade organizations have over the years developed some very sophisticated formulas all based on this principle. This simple formula works very well, particularly in areas such as computing, where there are no established formulas. Provided that the independent indexes are carefully selected as being representative of the materials and labor sector involved, the result is fairly accurate.

However, a few points need to be made. There may be an under- or overrecovery by Contractors if the formula is used on a Contract with a long time scale. By comparing the index at price base date with the index at the time of the claim, the pattern of increases or decreases during the period is ignored, and a false result may ensue. This problem can be mitigated by requiring claims to be submitted at intervals or by setting cutoff points for different components of the Contract Price, since not all cost components will be affected by price variations throughout the Contract period. Some will also argue that the percentages representing the cost components should not total 100 percent, since that includes profit, and the profit element should not be increased because of factors outside both the parties' control. The opposing view is that profit is a function of turnover and if, because of increases in costs, the rate of turnover increases, then profit should also increase. Another point is that you are unlikely to find any indexes under the heading of overheads; but since these include a fair proportion of general costs such as rent, rates, and services, the cost-of-living index can give a close enough result.

Now, after this involved explanation of the clause and the

way it can be applied, it must be pointed out that it has very limited application in the computer field, primarily because technological developments in computing are so rapid and there is so much price competition that manufacturers' list prices usually reflect a better cost-performance ratio as time progresses, notwithstanding worldwide inflation. So, at present, a Customer is probably better advised to accept manufacturers' list prices, which are increasing more slowly than national rates (many are even going down) than to apply the Variations in Cost Clause. However, the situation may change, and in the concept of Model Conditions, the clause is available if the Customer decides that the economic climate or his own particular needs justify its use. In most cases, it will be deleted, and fixed prices are obviously what the Customer should aim for.

Note that the formula does not have to be used against the total Contract Price. For instance, in the event that a large system is being developed by a manufacturer, his equipment supply may be excluded from the formula, but if a considerable proportion of costs is represented by the Contractor's labor, then this element can be covered on a formula basis.

CLAUSE 21. OWNERSHIP

21.1 The Equipment or any part thereof shall become the property of the Customer on payment of all sums due.

21.2 The Contractor's liability under Clause 18 shall, with respect to the Equipment or any part thereof, cease on the Acceptance Date of the Equipment or part thereof.

EXPLANATORY NOTES

This clause has caused a fair degree of dissension among the members of the IPS Working Party and opinions vary as to whether the clause should read as stated above or:

The Equipment or any part thereof shall become the property of the Customer on the issue of an Acceptance Certificate as under Clause 14.

Each version has merits and demerits and, as is the intention of Model Conditions, users can select whichever clause best suits their purpose.

Let us consider the clause which says that the property shall pass on the issue of the Acceptance Certificate. The argument there is that if, under Clause 19.1, there is a retention until the end of the Maintenance Period, then unless the property passes on acceptance, a susbstantial part of the Contract Price (usually 90 or 95 percent) will have been paid for which the Customer gets no property rights until he pays the small balance 12 months later.

However, as explained in the comments on Clause 19, the majority of purchase contracts for computer equipment will not require a retention, and 100 percent of the Contract Price will be paid after acceptance. This still leaves the 30 days (or whatever other period is agreed) between the issue of the Acceptance Certificate and payment, during which time the Equipment will be used for operational purposes.

This is clearly an area for agreement between the parties, and either clause makes for a workable contractual arrangement, particularly when allied with Clause 21.2, which defines when liability and insurance obligations expire.

CLAUSE 22. RECOVERY OF SUMS DUE

22.1 Whenever under the Contract any sum of money shall be recoverable from or payable by the Contractor, the same may be deducted from any sum then due or which at any time thereafter may become due to the Contractor under this or any other Contract with the Customer.

22.2 Exercise by the Customer of his rights under this Clause shall be without prejudice to any other rights or remedies available to the Customer under the Contract.

EXPLANATORY NOTES

The right of "offset"—that is, the right to deduct money from a Contractor on a Contract, against money he owes against any other Contract with the Customer—is not automatic, but it is thought to be equitable. This clause gives that right and confirms that the exercise of it does not prejudice any other rights under the Contract.

CLAUSE 23. WARRANTY PERIOD

23.1 The Contractor shall be responsible for correcting, with all possible speed and at his own expense, any defect in or damage to any portion of the Works which may develop during a period of 12 calendar months after the Acceptance Date (hereinafter referred to as "the Warranty Period"), for that portion which results in a failure of the Works to fulfill the functions or meet the level of performance detailed in the Contract or arises from *either:*

(i) Defective materials, including Software, workmanship, or design (other than a design furnished or specified by the Customer and for which the Contractor has disclaimed responsibility within a reasonable time after the receipt of the Customer's instructions); *or:*

(ii) Any act or omission of the Contractor during the Warranty Period.

23.2 If any such damage or defect is not remedied within a reasonable time, the Customer may proceed to do the work at the Contractor's risk and expense but without prejudice to any other rights which the Customer may have against the Contractor with respect to the failure of the Contractor to remedy such defect or damage.

23.3 Where a defect involves a fault inherent in the design of the Works, the Contractor shall at his own expense promptly carry out such redesign as may be necessary to prevent a recurrence of the defect and, upon completion of such redesign, shall rectify the fault in the Works. Any such redesign shall be accomplished in such a manner as to ensure that the performance and operation of the Works is not downgraded by virtue of such redesign from the standard as accepted by the Customer under Clause 13 (Acceptance Tests). The Warranty Period of 12 calendar months shall thereupon be renewed with respect to the Works or any portion thereof, subject to such redesign and rectification.

23.4 If the replacements or renewals are such that they may affect the performance of the Works or any portion thereof, the Customer may within one calendar month of such replacement or renewal give to the Contractor notice in writing requiring that the Acceptance Tests be made, in which case such tests shall be carried out as provided in Clause 13.

EXPLANATORY NOTES

The common practice of giving a period of warranty after the purchase of Equipment is followed generally by the computer industry, and in fact some manufacturers, particularly on mainframes, include a period of free maintenance in their price. This clause covers both situations, and details the remedies available to the Customer should the Contractor fail to carry out his obligations.

Subclause 23.1

This makes it clear that the Contractor is responsible for remedying with all possible speed (an important provision) any defects, arising from whatever cause, subject only to the exceptions discussed later. Although it specifies the period of warranty as 12 months, which is the normal practice, there is nothing sacrosanct about this period, and it may be extended or reduced by agreement between the parties. Indeed, some Contractors may decline to give any Warranty Period, in which case this will be a consideration in evaluating offers. With the development of diagnostic techniques, the location and identification of faults becomes easier, but we are still left with the very difficult problem of defining the reason for the failure of the Works to meet the level of performance detailed in the Contract. Provided the Acceptance Tests were properly designed to ensure proper performance, and if the Works passed those tests, then subsequent failure must be demonstrated by the Customer. If there is no obvious failure, or one that can be demonstrated by the diagnostic tools, then this demonstration is no easy task.

The exceptions referred to previously cover two situations. The first is in relation to any design furnished by the Customer, for which the Contractor has issued a disclaimer for that design. It may at first seem unreasonable to the Contractor to make him responsible for designs provided by the Customer unless he has specifically disclaimed responsibility, but on reflection it will be found to be equitable. The Contractor is the expert (that is why he has the Contract), and it is for him to tell the Customer if any designs he wants included are likely to affect performance. The second exception is where any action, or lack of action, by the Customer causes a failure: Clearly the Contractor cannot be held liable in these circumstances.

Subclause 23.2

In the comments on the previous subclause, attention was drawn to the importance of defects being remedied with all possible speed, and it is obvious that a Contractor's promises alone will not get the Customer's equipment back into operation. This subclause gives the Customer the right to call in someone else to rectify the fault and to charge the Contractor with the cost if he does not remedy the defects with all possible speed. The interpretation of what constitutes "all possible speed" must be reasonable, and impossible time scales must not be set. It will also be appreciated that where a retention sum is held under Clause 19 (Terms of Payment), this can be used for the purpose of paying another Contractor, but it is much more difficult to get money back from a Contractor that it is to deduct it from money owed to him.

Subclauses 23.3 and 23.4

These subclauses are likely to become operative only where the Contractor has to carry out a major redesign. In such cases, it will probably be necessary to prove that the redesigned Works will perform to the original standard, and Acceptance Tests will need to be rerun. A renewed Warranty Period should operate from the satisfactory completion of these tests on the portion of the Works affected.

CLAUSE 24. BANKRUPTCY

24.1 If the Contractor shall become bankrupt, or shall have a receiving order made against him or compound with his creditors, or, being a corporation, shall commence to be wound up (not being a member's voluntary closing down for the purpose of reconstruction or amalgamation) or to carry on its business under a receiver for the benefit of its creditors, the Customer shall be at liberty (a) to terminate the Contract forthwith by notice in writing to the Contractor, receiver, or liquidator, or to any person in whom the Contract may become vested, or (b) to give such receiver, liquidator, or other person the option of carrying out the Contract subject to his providing a guarantee for the due and faithful performance of the Contract up to an amount to be agreed.*

24.2 The Contractor shall, if any of the events in Subclause 24.1 become applicable, forthwith place in a bonded store or similar secure place, a copy of the relevant source coding and any other information or documentation necessary for the maintenance of the Software supplied under the Contract insofar as he is legally entitled to do so. In the event that it becomes necessary for the Customer to exercise his right of termination under Subclause 24.1, the source coding and

---

*This contents of Subclause 24.1 and the comments about it are particular to the United Kingdom, and no attempt has been made to adapt it to American practices. The reason for this is that most organizations and industries have their own Bankruptcy clauses and these, preferably in a shortened and simple form, will be suitable in place of the British version. The important and individual feature of this clause for computer Contracts is Subclause 24.2, where Customer protection for essential Software is covered.

other information or documentation shall immediately be handed over to the Customer free of any charge or encumbrance.

24.3 The exercise of rights under this clause shall not prejudice any existing rights or obligations of either party.

EXPLANATORY NOTES

To go bankrupt and have a receiver appointed is obviously the worst commercial situation that a Contractor can find himself in, but the effects on the Customer can also be traumatic. Receivers have wide-ranging legal powers, and a Contract may suddenly pass into the hands of someone who may be more concerned with winding up the company and gathering all the assets possible on behalf of the creditors than with protecting the interests of the Customer. In any event, the Customer needs all the protection that can be provided in the event of his Contractor's Bankruptcy, and a receiver will normally try to comply with protective clauses.

In the event of Bankruptcy, the receiver will usually consider whether it is possible for normal trading to continue, since this often offers the best chance for creditors to recover their money. If there are reasonable guarantees that the Contract can be performed, then it is usually best to arrange for its continuation, but if this is not possible, then the best course is probably to appoint another Contractor as quickly as possible. Subclause 24.1 gives the Customer the right to terminate the Contract and leaves him free to obtain his requirements from another source.

Subclause 24.1 is fairly normal in Model Conditions, and is adequate for most types of industry, but in computing there are the additional problems that Contractors often have source coding and other information and documentation, without which the Customer is seriously disadvantaged. Subclause 24.2 requires the Contractor to protect that source coding and information and to hand it over to the Customer if and when he exercises his right of termination of the Contract.

CLAUSE 25. STATUTORY AND OTHER REGULATIONS

25.1 The Contractor shall in all matters arising in the performance of the Contract conform with all Acts of Parliament* and with all orders, regulations, and bylaws made with statutory authority by government departments or by local or other authorities that shall be applicable to the Contract. The Contractor shall also observe through his staff people any rules applicable to the Premises where the Works are carried out. The Customer shall on request afford all reasonable assistance to the Contractor in obtaining information as to local conditions. In the performance of the Contract the Contractor shall not in any manner endanger the safety, or unlawfully interfere with the convenience, of the public. The cost to the Contractor in meeting the requirements of this Subclause shall be included in the Contract Price, except as provided under Subclause 25.4.

25.2. The Contractor shall give the Customer such prior written notice as the Customer may require of the delivery under the Contract of any goods having a toxic hazard or other hazard to the safety or health of persons or property, identifying those hazards and giving full details of any precautions to be taken by the Customer on the delivery of such goods and their subsequent storage or handling.

25.3 The Contractor shall ensure that all such goods are suitably packed and identified at the time of delivery with reference to the hazards connected with them.

*The legal structure in the United States, which allows federal, state, and local legislation to be applied to contracts, means that it would be presumptuous for anyone who is not an expert in American law to attempt to devise a clause to cover all American requirements. The British version is, therefore, included here as an example of the *type* of clause needed. Its specifics should be replaced by the normal statutory regulations clause operative in the Customer's locality. Attention is nevertheless drawn to the equitable nature of the British clause, and it is recommended that the three key points mentioned here be included in any statutory regulations clause.

25.4 If the cost to the Contractor of the performance of the Contract shall be increased or reduced by reason of the passage, after the date of the Contract, of any law, order, regulation, or bylaw having the force of law that shall be applicable to the Contract (other than any tax on profits or revenue), the amount of such increase or reduction shall be added to or deducted from the Contract Price.

25.5 In the event that the Contractor does not fulfill his responsibilities and obligations under the Contract and the Customer thereby incurs costs to which he would not otherwise be liable as a result of any law or order, regulation, or bylaw having the force of law, the amount of such costs shall be reimbursed by the Contractor to the Customer.

EXPLANATORY NOTES

This clause is perfectly straightforward and requires little explanation. There are only three points to make, and these summarize the content of the clause:

First, the Contractor must conform with all statutory and local authority regulations, as well as any rules applicable to the Premises. It is for the Customer to detail any such rules in his invitations to bid.

Second, if any additional rules and regulations are introduced after the Contract is placed, then the corresponding costs will be borne by the Customer.

Third, if the Contractor fails to fulfill his obligations, and this results in additional costs to the Customer which he would not have incurred had the Contractor fulfilled his obligations, then such additional costs shall be reimbursed to the Customer.

CLAUSE 26. WAIVER

No delay, neglect, or forbearance on the part of either party in enforcing against the other party any term or condition of the Contract shall either be, or be deemed to be, a waiver or in any way prejudice any right of that party under the Contract.

EXPLANATORY NOTES

This short clause is explicit, but an example may help. If under Subclause 11.3, the Contractor fails to give notice of his intention to make a claim within the 14 days allowed for this purpose, but the Customer subsequently agrees to meet his claim, it does not mean that the 14 days' notice shall not apply to any future instances.

CLAUSE 27. CONFIDENTIALITY

27.1 The Contractor and the Customer shall keep confidential any information obtained under the Contract and shall not divulge the same to any third party without the consent in writing of the other party.

27.2 The provisions of this Clause shall not apply to:

(i) Any information in the public domain otherwise than by breach of this Contract;

(ii) Information already in the possession of the receiving party;

(iii) Information obtained from a third party who is free to divulge the same.

27.3 The Contractor and the Customer shall divulge confidential information only to those employees who are directly involved in the Contract or in use of the Equipment and Software, and shall ensure that such employees are aware of and comply with their obligations as to Confidentiality.

27.4 The Contractor shall ensure that his Subcontractors are bound by the requirements of this Clause.

EXPLANATORY NOTES

Security of information is a much discussed topic in the computer field—and rightly so, because any data retrieval system will lay itself open to abuse if proper precautions are not taken.

In designing a system, and in writing Software, a Contractor is often given information about the Customer's operations, much of which could be of considerable value to a competitor. Similarly, the Customer may be given information about the Contractor's Equipment, manufacturing processes, or Software that would be valuable to his competitors. A Confidentiality clause is, therefore, highly desirable, if not essential.

The above clause is a simple one. It requires the consent in writing of the other party before one party can divulge any information provided under the Contract, except where such information is already in the public domain (usually through publication), is the existing property of the receiving party, or is obtained from a third party.

Subclause 27.3 requires both the Contractor and Customer to restrict confidential information under the Contract to those employees who are directly involved, and this can be a problem. Many firms require employees to sign undertakings of various kinds to ensure that they do not disclose confidential information, and in certain circumstances, particularly where government work is involved, firms screen potential employees. It is difficult to control individuals, especially when they leave the employment of the organizations involved, and this book is not the place for a detailed exposition of the potential problems and solutions. Let this warning suffice: A legal requirement is imposed on both parties (and any Subcontractors, as in Subclause 27.4) to take all reasonable precautions against disclosure.

CLAUSE 28. CONSUMABLE SUPPLIES

The Customer reserves the right to procure disks, magnetic tapes, paper tapes, punch cards, and any other Consumable Supplies to be used on and suitable for the Equipment from the Contractor or such other source as the Customer may deem appropriate, and such procurement from a source other than the Contractor shall not invalidate any rights of the Customer under these conditions.

EXPLANATORY NOTES

The Consumable Supplies referred to are the future operating supplies, such as punch cards, magnetic tapes, and disks, which do not form part of the Works.

The Customer will not want to be committed to the Contractor for the life of the Equipment for his Consumable Supplies, and it would be unreasonable for this to be expected. On the other hand, during the Warranty Period or under a maintenance agreement, the Contractor will not want to be involved in extra costs as a result of the Customer's using supplies which cause malfunction or deterioration of performance.

This clause, in conjunction with other clauses, is designed to strike the correct balance: It gives the Customer the right to use consumables obtained from sources other than the Contractor, and the Contractor is protected against having to meet additional costs in other related clauses. During the Warranty Period, Clause 23.1 restricts the Contractor's liability to failures or unsatisfactory performance arising from his own acts or omissions, and his own materials and Software. The exception contained in Clause 23.1 (i) relating to designs furnished or specified by the Customer has no relevance to consumable supplies obtained by him. Clause 16 (Standard of Performance) goes even further, in that it requires the Customer to demonstrate that any deterioration in performance is the fault of the Contractor—clearly not the case with consumables obtained by the Customer elsewhere.

If there is a separate Maintenance Contract, the liabilities of parties will be specified under that Contract, and that aspect is dealt with under the following clause.

CLAUSE 29. MAINTENANCE

If required by the Customer, the Contractor shall enter into a separate Contract with the Customer for Maintenance of the Equipment or any part thereof at any time after the Acceptance Date for a specific time period and on terms and conditions to be agreed between the Customer and the Contractor.

EXPLANATORY NOTES

This clause gives the Customer the right to require the Contractor to enter into a separate Maintenance Contract for the Equipment supplied under the Contract. Most Contractors are happy to enter into such a Contract, but what is the position if the Contractor is not prepared to maintain the Equipment?

The inclusion of the clause in the request for proposals is the trigger for the Contractor to assess his position, and if he is not prepared to enter into a Maintenance Contract, then he must say so in his offer. If this is the case, the Customer will take that into consideration when evaluating the offers. If he proceeds with the Contractor who has declined to provide a maintenance service, and if the Contract is placed on the basis of the Contractor's offer, then the provisions of this clause will not apply.

If it is decided to proceed with a separate Maintenance Contract, then at this stage the Customer will almost certainly be faced with a form of agreement prepared by the Contractor, and this document should be examined very carefully to ensure that it is equitable and that any hard-won remedies under the supply Contract are not given away in the Maintenance Contract.

At the time this book was first published, the IPS Working Group was working on Model Conditions of Contract for the Maintenance of Computer Equipment, which will supplement the Conditions of Purchase. It is hoped that these will be available shortly. Until then the Customer should consider the reasons for the inclusion of the protective clauses in the Conditions of Purchase, and try to extend the same rationale to his maintenance contract.

To pick up the point on consumables in Clause 28, any contract for maintenance should also give the Customer the right to obtain his own consumables, but in equity it must also state that if the use of these involves the Contractor in any additional maintenance costs, then these will be reimbursed to him by the Customer.

CLAUSE 30. SPARES
30.1 The Contractor shall use his best efforts to maintain for the Equipment a supply of spares or replacement parts for a period of ten years from the Acceptance Date, such spares or replacement parts to be fully compatible with, but not necessarily identical to, similar items previously supplied.
30.2 If, during the period of ten years referred to in Sub-clause 30.1, the Contractor intends to discontinue the manufacture of spares or replacement parts for the Equipment, the Contractor shall forthwith give notice to the Customer of such intention, and shall afford the Customer the opportunity (which should be exercised within three months) of ordering at reasonable prices such quantities of spares or replacement parts as the Customer shall reasonably require in relation to the anticipated life of the Equipment. Alternatively, the parties may agree with the said period of three months upon a price at which the Contractor will sell to the Customer such drawings, patterns, specifications, and other information as he may have in his possession and as the Customer shall require to enable him to make or have made such spares or replacement parts.
30.3 If, during the above-mentioned period of ten years, the Contractor (in the absence of agreement as aforesaid) fails to fulfill an order for the supply of spares or replacement parts given by the Customer, or, not having given notice as

aforesaid, *either* (a) fails to make available to the Customer with reasonable dispatch and at reasonable prices all such spares or replacement parts as the Customer shall require for the Equipment; *or* (b) becomes insolvent or bankrupt and commences to close down (not being a member's voluntary closing down for the purpose of reconstruction), then the Contractor shall, as far as he is legally entitled to do, and if so required by the Customer, as soon as reasonably practicable deliver to the Customer free of charge such drawings, patterns, specifications, and other information as are referred to in Subclause 30.2, which the Customer shall be entitled to retain for such time only as is necessary for the Customer to exercise his rights under this Clause, and which, if the Contractor so requires, shall be returned by the Customer to the Contractor in good order and condition (fair wear and tear excepted) and at the Customer's cost and expense.

30.4 If the Customer shall exercise his right under Subclause 30.3 of this Clause, the Contractor shall also grant to the Customer, without payment of any royalty or charge, full right and liberty to make or have made spares or replacement parts as aforesaid and for such purposes only to use, make, and have made copies of all drawings, patterns, specifications, and other information supplied by the Contractor to the Customer, pursuant to the Contract.

30.5 The Customer undertakes for himself and on behalf of his employees and agents that all drawings, patterns, specifications, and other information obtained from the Contractor under this Clause shall be kept confidential and will not be divulged except to such persons as it may be necessary to divulge the same to for the purpose of making or having made spares or replacement parts as aforesaid.

30.6 The Contractor will, as far as he is reasonably able, bind his Subcontractors to conform with the requirements of this Clause, and prior to entry into any such Subcontract, provide the Customer with full details of any Subcontractor who will not so conform, in which event the Customer may direct the Contractor to seek an alternative Subcontractor. Any additional costs incurred by the Contractor in placing any such Subcontract with an alternative Subcontractor shall be added to the Contract Price.

30.7 If the Contractor fails to provide spares or replacement parts as described in Subclause 30.3, and if these are available from his Subcontractor, the Customer shall have the right to obtain such spares and replacement parts from the Subcontractor or any other supplier, and any additional cost incurred by the Customer shall be recoverable from the Contractor.

EXPLANATORY NOTES

When a user buys a computer system, he is usually making a reasonably long-term investment, particularly if he has chosen a system that is capable of being extended to meet his future needs. This being the case, the last thing he wants to find is that spares are unavailable for the Maintenance of the Equipment, and this clause is designed to make provision against that eventuality.

Subclause 30.1

This is a "best efforts" type of clause and requires the Contractor to do his best to protect the interests of his Customer over a period of ten years. It would be ideal from the Customer's viewpoint if he could put an absolute requirement on the Contractor to supply such spares or replacement parts as are required over a period of ten years, but this would not be equitable, and manufacturers would find it unacceptable. The subclause recognizes that technical developments will occur during such a long period, and accepts that the spares and replacement parts need not be identical to the original components, as long as they are compatible.

Subclause 30.2

Because Subclause 30.1 is a "best efforts" clause, there is no compulsion on the Contractor to continue to supply spares and replacement parts, but if during that period he intends to discontinue supply, then the Customer will want to be able to obtain the items he thinks will be needed to cover the expected life of the Equipment, or to arrange for supply from another source.

If the Contractor gives notice of discontinuance, then the exercise of the first of the options by the Customer will cause some difficulty, for it requires him to anticipate the requirements of spares and replacement parts, possibly over a period of several years. The better course would be to negotiate the acquisition of the drawings and specifications, to enable him to arrange his own future supplies.

Subclauses 30.3 and 30.4

If the Contractor does not give notice of discontinuance under Subclause 30.2, but fails to supply the Customer's requirements, then this is presumably because he has particular supply difficulties or because he either has ceased or will be ceasing to trade. In either event, the Customer still needs to obtain his spares and replacement parts, and the Contractor is required to supply drawings and specifications to enable the Customer to obtain his spares elsewhere.

Subclause 30.5

If, under the preceding two subclauses, the Contractor supplies information to the Customer, he will want him to observe confidentiality, and the Customer is required to take all steps to preserve this confidentiality.

Subclause 30.6

At first sight, this subclause seems to place an onerous burden on the Contractor, but on reflection it will be seen that it is in the Contractor's own interests to ensure that his Subcontractors comply with the previous requirements of the clause.

The Contractor will undoubtedly have a major investment at stake when he launches a new range of Equipment, and he stands to suffer most if his Subcontractor fails to supply parts for his manufacture. Provisions in his Contract with the Subcontractor to ensure that parts are available either from him or from another source during manufacture are essential, and the extension of this requirement for a reasonable period should cause no undue difficulties.

Subclause 30.7

This last subclause gives the Customer the right to go direct to the Subcontractor or any other supplier, if the Contractor fails to supply spares and replacement parts normally obtained from that source. The provision for additional costs to be recovered from the Contractor should not apply in normal trading circumstances, since the Customer would not expect to pay the Contractor's administrative charges and profit on the Subcontractor's price. The price direct from a Subcontractor is normally lower than where supply is through the main Contractor, and the same should be true for spares and replacement parts supplied by another components manufacturer.

CLAUSE 31. SOFTWARE

31.1 Unless otherwise stated in the Contract, the Contractor shall be responsible for providing in accordance with the Contract all Software and associated documentation necessary for the satisfactory operation of the Equipment.

31.2 With regard to any Software developed by the Contractor specifically for the Contract, the title thereto shall vest in the Contractor, but the Contractor shall grant to the Customer the free and unrestricted right to use and modify such Software for his own use.

31.3 With regard to any Software supplied under the Contract over which the Contractor or third parties hold title or other rights, the Contractor shall permit or procure for the Customer (as the case may require) the right to use and apply that Software free of additional charge (together with any modifications, improvements, and developments thereof) in the operation of the Equipment and in the operation of other computers owned or used by the Customer.

31.4 With regard to any Software such as is referred to in Subclause 31.3 above, the Customer undertakes not to disclose or make available any part or parts thereof to any third party without the prior written consent of the Contractor.

31.5 The Contractor's permission referred to in Subclause 31.3 shall be given (*inter alia*) to enable the Customer to disclose (under conditions of Confidentiality satisfactory to the Contractor) programs and documentation for a third party to undertake the performance of services for the Customer with respect to such programs and documentation.

31.6 In addition to his obligations under Clause 23, the Contractor shall provide Software maintenance services as defined in the Contract.

31.7 If, in meeting his obligations under Subclause 31.6, the Contractor for his own purposes modifies any of the Software supplied under the Contract, and if such modification adversely affects the level of performance of the Equipment and Software, then the Contractor shall, at his own expense, provide such items of Equipment as may be necessary to return the level of performance of the Equipment and Software to that specified in the Contract.

31.8 The Customer shall make only as many copies of the Software or any portion thereof as are reasonably necessary for operational security and use.

31.9 The Customer reserves the right to use other software on the Equipment supplied under this Contract.

EXPLANATORY NOTES

This clause is potentially the most sensitive in the Model Conditions, and what is included is not incompatible with the concept of "unbundling" and program product licenses. At the same time, it recognizes the requirements of the Customer. The intent to achieve equity has probably been realized, as evidenced by comments made by both Contractors and users that the clause is biased in the other's favor!

The reader can judge for himself in the light of the comments on each subclause, but users of the Model Conditions are again reminded that they are written to cover the *majority* of circumstances and to be compatible with general practices; clauses can always be deleted or substituted to meet special circumstances.

Subclause 31.1

There is a great deal of inconsistency in the use of terminology in the computer field, and in common usage this subclause requires the Contractor to provide operating Software with his Equipment. However, in these days of microcoding and "wired-in" instructions, it might be incomplete to leave the description just as operating Software. The clause is carefully worded to require the Contractor to provide "all Software and associated documentation for the satisfactory operation of the Equipment": The Customer wants everything necessary to enable him to operate the Equipment, in accordance with the Contract.

Subclause 31.2

In almost every contractual situation, the buyer has the right to say that if he is paying for something in a Contract, then he should have the resultant title. In computing, however, this is not necessarily so, and Software is an example of this exception.

Even where specially commissioned, Software is usually written on the basis of other Software which has already been developed by, and is the property of, the Contractor, and it is very difficult to argue in the general case that the Customer is paying the entire cost of the resultant Software. In view of this, the best that could be argued from the Customer's viewpoint is that the rights should be shared, but such an arrangement is seldom satisfactory from either party's point of view.

Much of the business of Contractors, particularly the Software specialists, is based on their background expertise and titles to existing Software. Unless a Customer is interested in the exploitation of Software, he will usually get a better commercial deal by negotiating a Contract on the basis of the Contractor's retaining the title, but with completely free and unrestricted use for his own purposes. This subclause reflects that belief. However, if the Customer wishes to obtain sole rights to Software for which he is paying all the costs, and which he might wish to exploit or protect from competitors, then the subclause should be amended to reflect that situation.

Subclause 31.3

This subclause is based on the same philosophy as the previous subclauses and on the belief that the Customer's interests are best served by having free and unrestricted use of all the Software supplied under the Contract. Where the Contractor is unable to obtain this freedom of use for the Customer with respect to Software owned by a third party, then this must be stated in the offer, and an evaluation of the resulting additional costs and constraints will have to be made by the Customer. If this situation applies, then the clause will need to be amended.

Subclause 31.4

Once again, the need for confidentiality is reflected, and in this case it is for the Customer to ensure that there is no disclosure without the written consent of the Contractor.

Subclause 31.5

As part of the Customer's operational requirements, he may require other services (including the provision of special Software application packages) from third parties, and the use of the Software as required under Subclause 31.3 can be required to be extended in connection with other services provided by a third party. The only problem this may cause is if the Contractor has some specific reason for wanting to preserve the Confidentiality of his Software. If the Contractor has a general objection to the use of his Software for such purposes, then he should state this in his offer. Otherwise, the Customer will be entitled to expect that Confidentiality objections will be raised only for specific reasons.

Subclause 31.6

Most Contractors will provide Software services such as updating and fault rectification as a matter of course, and their price for Software will state the terms under which this service is provided. It is an essential requirement which Customers should ensure is available.

Subclause 31.7

In the final analysis, the primary interest of the Customer is in the performance of the Equipment and Software for his operational purposes, and if the Contractor amends his Software in any way which results in a deterioration of that performance, then the Customer will want the position rectified. This subclause places that obligation on the Contractor, who, if necessary, must supplement the Equipment to provide the necessary level of performance.

Subclause 31.8

As part of the confidentiality aspect, the Customer should not proliferate copies of the Software supplied under the Contract. This subclause makes that constraint clear.

Subclause 31.9

This last subclause merely ensures that the Customer has the right to use other Software on the Equipment supplied under the Contract.

CLAUSE 32. FORCE MAJEURE

Neither party shall be liable for failure to perform its obligations under the Contract if such failure results from circumstances beyond the party's reasonable control.

EXPLANATORY NOTES

A claim for force majeure may be obvious in some cases—wars, riots, insurrections, or acts of God, for example. Other circumstances may not be so clear, and in these cases it is often a matter for the lawyers to determine.

In essence the clause is sensible and equitable in that if either of the parties is prevented from carrying out his obligations by a major force, then he should not be penalized for his failure. In practice, force majeure is often claimed when there is no real justification for it.

CLAUSE 33. ATTACHMENTS TO THE EQUIPMENT

The Customer shall have the right to attach to the Equipment free of charge any Equipment not supplied by the Contractor. The Customer shall notify the Contractor in writing of the intention to make such attachment, and it shall be a duty of the Contractor to notify the Customer forthwith if he has or subsequently receives any information to show that such attachment is or could be detrimental to the efficient operation of the Equipment.

In the event that the attachment is made by the Customer, and if the Contractor can prove that such attachment is adversely affecting the Equipment, then the Contractor shall be entitled to be relieved of his obligations under Clause 23 and to be reimbursed any associated costs which he can prove have arisen as a result of the attachment.

EXPLANATORY NOTES

This clause is really a counter to a clause which has in the past been included in many computer manufacturers' Conditions of Sale, and which said that the Customer was prohibited from attaching other manufactures' Equipment to his own without permission to do so. Such permission often carried an additional cost to the Customer.

This clause enables the Customer to attach other manufactures' Equipment to that supplied under the Contract, but requires him to inform the Contractor of his intention. It is then the duty of the Contractor to inform the Customer if he thinks such attachments could be detrimental to the performance of the Equipment.

If no such notification is given to the Customer, then he is entitled to think that the attachment he makes will not be detrimental, but it is recognized that the Contractor cannot test all the Equipment available form other sources and may not recognize that an attachment could prove detrimental. The last part of the clause, therefore, provides that the Customer shall pay for any extra costs incurred by the Contractor during the Warranty Period where the Contractor can prove that such extra costs are a result of the Customer's attachments.

If a separate maintenance contract is negotiated, a similar clause should be inserted.

CLAUSE 34. TRAINING
The Contractor shall provide instruction in the use of the Equipment and Software for the Customer's personnel in

accordance with the requirements of the Contract. Unless otherwise specified, no charge shall be made for such instruction, but the Customer shall be responsible for paying any travel or living expenses necessarily incurred by the Customer's personnel attending such instruction. If the extent of such instruction is not detailed in the Contract, the Contractor shall provide adequate instruction for a sufficient number of the Customer's personnel to secure the satisfactory operation of the Equipment and Software.

EXPLANATORY NOTES

Most Contractors provide in their quoted price for a certain amount of instruction to Customers' employees to enable them to operate the Equipment supplied under the Contract. Where the details of this provision are not spelled out, or where there is no inclusion for training in the Contract Price, but the customer expects training to be provided free of charge, then difficulties arise.

To obviate such difficulties, it is initially up to the Customer to specify his requirements for training in the invitation to bid and, in accordance with this clause, the Contractor will price these requirements and allow for them in his Contract Price. If, however, the Customer fails to specify his requirements, the Contractor is required to provide in his price for "adequate instruction for a sufficient number of the Customer's personnel to ensure the satisfactory operation of the Equipment and Software." Although this ensures that there is no total misunderstanding of what is included in the Contract Price, it is only a matter of degree, and each party may have an entirely different view of what is "adequate." In the absence of any statement of the Customer's requirements, it is strongly recommended that the Contractor detail exactly what provision he has made: It will probably save much argument and any deterioration of relationships.

The clause also makes it clear that the Customer will be responsible for traveling and living expenses of his personnel who attend the training sessions.

CLAUSE 35. PUBLICITY

Neither the Contractor nor his Subcontractor(s) shall without the prior written consent of the Customer advertise or publicly announce that he is undertaking work for the Customer.

EXPLANATORY NOTES

Computer manufacturers are usually glad to publicize important Contracts, particularly with prestige Customers, but the Customer may for a number of reasons wish to avoid publicizing the Contract. This clause is a standard provision, requiring the written consent of the Customer to publication.

CLAUSE 36. OPERATING MANUALS

The Contractor shall supply to the Customer all Operating Manuals and other documentation to be supplied in accordance with the Contract. The Customer reserves the right to withhold payment for that part of the Works for which an Acceptance Certificate has been issued but for which such manuals and documentation have not been supplied. The Contractor shall use his best efforts to update and replace where appropriate—and at reasonable prices—all such Operating Manuals and documentation for a period of ten years after the Acceptance Date.

EXPLANATORY NOTES

Operating Manuals are essential for a Customer's normal operating purposes, and, notwithstanding the issue of an Acceptance Certificate with respect to the Equipment, he might well be inhibited in its operational use without the manuals. For this reason, the Customer is entitled to withhold payment for that part of the Works for which Operating Manuals have not been supplied.

As far as updating and replacement of manuals is concerned, the situation is similar to that of spares (Clause 30), and once again, for the reasons given in discussing that clause, a " best efforts" clause is included for operating Manuals.

CLAUSE 37. ARBITRATION

Except where otherwise provided, if any dispute or difference arises between the Customer and the Contractor in connection with or arising out of the Contract, and provided that either of them shall have given to the other notice in writing thereof, such dispute or difference shall be referred to a single arbitrator to be agreed between the Customer and the Contractor or, failing such agreement, within 14 days from receipt of such notice in writing to be nominated by the American Arbitration Association on the application of either party, and any such reference will be deemed to be a submission for Arbitration.

EXPLANATORY NOTES

These Conditions of Contract, like most other conditions, contain the word "reasonable" in a number of places, but even without this inclusion, it is incumbent on both parties to act in a reasonable manner. Unfortunately, that which is reasonable to one party does not always appear reasonable to the other, and disputes can arise. In these cases, the parties may have recourse to Arbitration and litigation.

This clause details the arrangements for the appointment of an arbitrator, either by mutual agreement or through the agency of the American Arbitration Association, which is a nonprofit organization specifically established to provide an impartial forum for arbitration of all types of disputes.

Arbitration and litigation should only be undertaken reluctantly and as a very last resort. If the parties could agree to a mutually acceptable independent body or person acting as an unofficial arbitrator in an informal manner, or if they agree to follow the European pattern, with each side appointing an arbitrator, who in turn appoints a third arbitrator (once more acting informally), then much time and money might be saved by both parties.

CLAUSE 38. LAW*

Unless otherwise agreed in writing between the parties, the Contract shall be subject to and construed and interpreted in accordance with English Law, and shall be subject to the jurisdiction of the Courts of England.

EXPLANATORY NOTES

The equitable nature of these conditions should make them broadly acceptable in any country, but once more, a last-resort procedure for disputes needs to be agreed upon, and this needs to accord with national laws.

For instance, if an American company is manufacturing in Scotland and is supplying to a French national based in England, it is just as well to stipulate which national laws should apply in the event of litigation.

---

*As in the case of Clause 25, Statutory and Other Regulations, no attempt has been made to adopt the "Law" clause to suit American requirements, and the original British clause is included merely as an example.

The original two paragraphs of explanatory notes above are also retained in their original form, since the principles are equally valid in Great Britain or the United States. With the increase in international trading, particularly in the computing field, a simple clause stating which country or state shall exert jurisdiction over the Contract is strongly recommended.

Appendix to model form of conditions of contract for the supply and installation (purchase) of computer equipment

Clause 11.1 Delays by the Contractor
Percentage of the Contract Price to be deducted as damages for each week of delay between the agreed Completion Date and the actual Acceptance Date: _____%
Maximum percentage of the Contract Price which the deductions may not exceed: _____%

Clause 18.4 Indemnity and Insurance
The liability of the Contractor to the Customer under Subclause 18.1 with respect to any one act or default shall not exceed: $_____

Clause 19.1 Terms of Payment
Percentage of the Contract Price to be paid on the issue of an Acceptance Certificate under Clause 14: _____%

Explanatory Note: The way in which this Appendix should be used, and advice on the figures to be inserted, are given in the explanatory notes to the individual clauses, and reference should be made to them.

5

Shortened form of model form of conditions of contract for the supply and installation (purchase) of computer equipment

The Model Form of Conditions is, as should be appreciated by now, a very extensive set of clauses designed to cover every circumstance, including some that will only rarely apply, such as the Factory Tests Clause.

Where the Customer requires a complicated configuration or a costly and elaborate system, he will want to get the protection that these clauses give him, but the IPS Working Party recognized that most orders are for small computers and peripherals of the standard catalog variety supplied by the manufacturer, plugged in, and then subject to a six- or twelve-month warranty period. In other words, the process is almost like buying any other piece of office equipment, except that even in these simpler circumstances, there are specific points of protection required by the Customer.

The usual situation is that the Customer is once more confronted with the manufacturers' Conditions of Sale which protect the manufacturer very well but leave the Customer largely unprotected. Customers often try to overcome this difficulty by trying to impose their own Conditions of Purchase, but these are seldom satisfactory, since they have not been designed to cover the peculiarities of computerized equipment.

To fill this void, the Working Party has produced a Shortened Form of the Model Conditions, which is a simplified version of the main Conditions but covers all the normal requirements for the purchase of minor items of computerized equipment. As before, the reader will be taken through the individual clauses, but if there are requirements that are not covered in the Shortened Form, then the relevant clause from the Main Conditions can be added. Or, if the Customer thinks that a shortened clause needs amplification in a special circumstance, then the full clause from the Main Conditions should be quoted.

CLAUSE 1. DEFINITIONS

1.1 "Customer" shall mean _____
whose principal office is at _____
and shall include the Customer's legal personal representatives, successors, and assigns.

1.2 "Contractor" shall mean the person, firm, or company whose offer has been accepted by the Customer, and shall include the Contractor's personal representatives, successors, and permitted assigns.

1.3 "Contract" shall mean the agreement between the Customer and the Contractor, including all documents to which reference may properly be made in order to ascertain the rights and obligations of the parties.

1.4 "Equipment" shall mean all materials, plant, and hardware supplied by the Contractor under the Contract.

1.5 "Contract Price" shall mean the sum so named in the Contract, together with any additions thereto or deductions therefrom agreed in writing under the Contract.

1.6 "Premises" shall mean the place or places other than the Contractor's premises to which the Equipment is to be delivered or where the work is to be done described under the Contract.

EXPLANATORY NOTES

An explanation has already been given for those definitions where comment was considered necessary in discussing the Main Conditions, and no purpose would be served in repeating it here. Rather, the opportunity will be taken to explain why some definitions have been omitted. This will assist in understanding the rationale behind the Shortened Form.

The definitions that have been omitted from the Shortened Form are:

Works. The definitions of Works is an all-embracing description covering installation, testing, and setting to work of Equipment and Software. This definition is much wider than is required for the simple supply and delivery (perhaps not even tested on site by the Contractor) of small standard catalog-type items.

Software. Much of the Equipment supplied against the Shortened Form will be "slave" items of equipment where the software is contained in the "master" equipment. Even where the Contract involves "intelligent" terminals containing software, the software is likely to be fairly simple and probably "wired in," and is not likely to need definition of ownership or license.

Contracting Officer. Where only straightforward supply and delivery are involved, it is unlikely that site instructions will need to be issued; hence, the absence of the officer responsible.

Subcontractor. Once more in the supply and delivery of catalog-type equipment, it is highly unlikely that a specialist Subcontractor will be employed.

Program of Works. A detailed program covering stages of activities is not needed in a simple supply and delivery situation, but the Customer must ensure that he gets a firm delivery date for inclusion in the Contract.

Factory Tests. It is unlikely that factory tests will be required for standard catalog-type equipment.

Acceptance Tests. The Equipment supplied under a supply and delivery type of contract will still need to be tested when received, even if this test consists merely of plugging the item in to ensure that it works. What is unlikely to be needed is a protracted series of specially defined tests carried out by the Contractor in the presence of the Customer. It is more likely that the Customer will merely check the Equipment for himself.

Completion Date. This is the date upon which the Works should have passed all the Acceptance Tests and be ready for operational use. In large contracts that include inspection, testing, and setting to work, the Completion Date is often some time after the programmed date for delivery. With a simple supply and delivery contract, it is the delivery date that is important, since small items of Equipment are usually plugged in and ready for operational use almost immediately.

Acceptance Date. This is the date when all Acceptance Tests have been satisfactorily completed; it follows that if there are no formal Acceptance Tests, then no Acceptance Date needs to be included in the Shortened Form Conditions.

CLAUSE 2. THE PREMISES
Preparation and Provision
2.1 The Contractor shall supply adequate information in reasonable time to enable the Customer to provide adequate environmental and operational conditions for the Equipment, and the Customer shall suitably prepare the Premises prior to the delivery and installation of the Equipment.
2.2 Any reasonable additional costs incurred by the Con-

tractor because of the Customer's failure to prepare the Premises suitably (except where such failure results from the Contractor's failure to comply with Clause 2.1) shall be done by the Customer.

2.3 *Access.* The Customer shall, with his prior agreement, provide such reasonable access to the Premises as the Contractor may require for the purposes of the Contract.

EXPLANATORY NOTES

This clause is a shortened version of two clauses in the Main Conditions, those dealing with the Premises and Access.

The part of the clause in the Shortened Form dealing with the Premises is very similar to that in the Main Conditions, and no amplification is needed to the explanations given of the Main Conditions clause, but the part relating to Access is very much abbreviated compared with the Main Conditions clause.

It will be noted that there is no provision for the removal of any of the Contractor's personnel in the event that they are deemed not to be "a fit and proper person to be on the Premises." This is because there is unlikely to be more than a very short-term delivery and connection operation to be performed by the Contractors' people. The chances are that they will have done their job and left the premises before any real opinion can be formed.

The other main omission from the Shortened Form is the security aspect. Once more, the fact that little more than a delivery service is likely to be provided on small plug-in items of Equipment was taken into account. If there are any Access restrictions, then these must be spelled out to the Contractor in the invitation to bid.

CLAUSE 3. MISTAKES IN INFORMATION

The Contractor and the Customer shall each be responsible for the accuracy of drawings, documentation, and information supplied by them to the other party and shall pay to the other party any extra costs occasioned by any discrepancies, errors, or omissions therein.

EXPLANATORY NOTES

Once again, this is a simplified version of the clause in the Main Conditions, and the same comments apply.

CLAUSE 4. INSPECTION, TESTING, AND ACCEPTANCE

4.1 The Contractor shall complete all agreed Inspection and Testing of the Equipment prior to dispatch or at the Customer's Premises, as required by the Contract.

4.2 When the Equipment has been delivered and installed in accordance with the Contract and has passed all agreed Inspection and Testing required under the Contract, it will be accepted by the Customer.

EXPLANATORY NOTES

This Shortened Form clause again reflects the type of Equipment to which these conditions are intended to apply, as well as the general practice of the trade. Manufacturers will normally ensure that the Equipment is in good working order when it leaves the factory, and they do this by carrying out a series of tests on individual components during manufacture and by performance tests on completed Equipment, usually on specifically designed test rigs.

Equipment is, therefore, expected to be in good working order when it leaves the factory, and performance should meet the specification published by the manufacturer. However, the Equipment may not be in good working order when received by the Customer, and the most common reason for this is damage in transit. Furthermore, the Equipment may not meet the performance standard required by the Customer, and where such performance was the basis of the Contractor's offer, then the Contractor has the obligation to meet the performance criteria included in the Contract before it is accepted by the Customer.

CLAUSE 5. EXTENSION OF TIME FOR COMPLETION

If the Contractor is delayed in completing the Contract by any act or omission of the Customer or by any circumstances beyond the Contractor's reasonable control, and shall without delay notify the Customer of such delay, then the Customer shall grant the Contractor such extension of time as may be reasonable.

EXPLANATORY NOTES

This Shortened Form of the main clause is intended to operate in exactly the same way as that in the main clause, and the same explanations apply.

CLAUSE 6. DELAYS IN COMPLETION

If the Contractor fails to complete the Contract by the agreed completion date, or such extended date as may be granted by the Customer under Clause 5, the Customer shall be entitled to deduct as liquidated damages for delay 1 percent of the total Contract Price for every week's delay, up to a minimum of 10 percent.

EXPLANATORY NOTES

The rationale for this liquidated damages clause is the same as that for the equivalent clause in the Main Conditions, except that the Shortened Form states the amount of damages that will be deducted in the event of delays for which the Contractor is liable.

The figures included are a reasonable norm, and enable the Contractor to evaluate and price his risk. If, however, the Customer does not consider that the figures reflect a reasonable assessment of the losses he will suffer in the event of delayed delivery, then the figures can be amended. Provided that they are not penal and are accepted by the Contractor, they become a valid contractual inclusion.

This does not cover the situation where no losses will be incurred by the Customer in the event of delayed delivery, and this is why most Customers object to the position adopted by many manufacturers of refusing to give a firm, guaranteed delivery date.

A Customer orders Equipment only on the assumption that he will obtain benefit from it (he should not order it otherwise), although with small items he is unlikely to go to the trouble of performing an extensive cost-benefit analysis. The precise extent of his losses are, therefore, unlikely to be available, but they will occur, and the figures shown are, as was previously stated, a reasonable norm.

CLAUSE 7. PATENTS, DESIGNS, AND COPYRIGHT

The Contractor shall indemnify the Customer against all claims, damages, costs, and expenses claimed or incurred by reason of any infringement of patents, designs, or copyright by the Customer's use or possession of the Equipment supplied under the Contract.

EXPLANATORY NOTES

The essence of this Shortened Form of the clause in the Main Conditions is in no way different, but it does not specify any mechanism for dealing with infringement. The mechanisms in the main clause are eminently sensible, and it is recommended that they be followed.

Shortened Form of Model Form

CLAUSE 8. ASSIGNMENT AND SUBLETTING
Except where otherwise provided by the Contract, the Contractor shall not assign, pledge, transfer, or sublet the Contract or any part thereof without the prior written consent of the Customer.

EXPLANATORY NOTES

This Shortened Form clause is basically the same as the clause in the Main Conditions. Once more, it is not intended to restrict the Contractor in relation to buying materials or components for the Equipment to be supplied.

CLAUSE 9. LIABILITY FOR ACCIDENT AND DAMAGE
9.1 The Contractor shall indemnify the Customer against and insure against injury (including death) to any person or loss of or damage to any property which arises out of the act, default, or negligence of the Contractor, his agents, or Subcontractors, or by reason of defective design or workmanship in the Contractor's Equipment.

9.2 The Contractor shall not be liable to the Customer for:
(i) Damage to Equipment or injury to persons resulting from improper use or handling of the Equipment by the Customer, his employees,or his agents;
(ii) Any loss of profit or Contracts or other consequential losses contingent on the said damage or injury.

EXPLANATORY NOTES

The concepts of indemnity and insurance are often improperly understood by people not dealing regularly with these matters, and in the use of this clause, it is recommended that the comments against the clause in the Main Conditions be considered.

The Shortened Form of the main clause is exactly the same in concept, and states the Contractor's obligations and the exceptions thereto. The Customer's obligations are implied rather than stated positively, but from the Contractor's viewpoint, it is sufficient to enable him to define his own risks accurately and to include them in his Contract Price.

There is no specific requirement for the Contractor to insure against his indemnity, since it is assumed that his obligations under this clause will be covered by his normal "all risks" policy.

CLAUSE 10. TERMS OF PAYMENT
The Contract Price shall become due for payment when the Equipment has been accepted in accordance with Clause 4.2. Payment will be made within 30 days of receipt by the Customer of a correct invoice from the Contractor.

EXPLANATORY NOTES

This is a simple clause, but payment periods can be amended by mutual agreement to suit the requirements of Customer or Contractor. The one point that Customers should bear in mind is that, in the evaluation of offers, differing payment period proposals should be priced and taken into account.

CLAUSE 11. OWNERSHIP
The Equipment shall become the property of the Customer on payment of all sums due.

EXPLANATORY NOTES

This clause recognizes the current practice of the trade with respect to small items of equipment.

Shortened Form of Model Form

CLAUSE 12. WARRANTY PERIOD

The Contractor shall be responsible for correcting, with all possible speed and at his own expense, any defect in or damage to the Equipment or to any portion thereof which may develop during a period of 12 months after acceptance (hereinafter referred to as the "Warranty Period") which results from:

(i) Defective materials (including Software), workmanship, design (other than a design furnished or specified by the Customer and for which the Contractor has disclaimed responsibility within a reasonable time after receipt of the Customer's instructions); *or*

(ii) Any act or omission of the Contractor during the Warranty Period.

EXPLANATORY NOTES

This Shortened Form clause differs from the clause in the Main Conditions in that it does not detail how the Customer may rectify the situation where the Contractor fails to remedy faults during the Warranty Period. This reflects the practical difficulties the Customer may face if there is no retention money held.

If the Customer holds no Contractor's monies, then his only redress is to sue for breach of contract, but such an extreme action is unlikely to occur with respect to minor items of equipment. The situation may be different if a large number of these items are purchased on one Contract. In such a case, it is recommended that the full clause from the Main Conditions be used and that retention monies be considered.

CLAUSE 13. BANKRUPTCY

If the Contractor shall become bankrupt or make an arrangement with his creditors to go into liquidation, the Customer shall have the right to terminate the Contract forthwith.

EXPLANATORY NOTES

The rationale behind this Shortened Form clause is that, in the purchase of minor and peripheral equipment, there are usually many alternatives available to the user, and in the event of the Bankruptcy of the Contractor, then the Customer wants to be free immediately to pursue an alternative source of supply.

CLAUSE 14. STATUTORY AND OTHER REGULATIONS*

The Contractor shall comply at his own expense with all Acts of Parliament and all statutory orders, regulations, and by-laws applicable to the Contract. The Contractor shall also observe at his own expense all regulations applicable to the Premises, details of which will be provided by the Customer.

EXPLANATORY NOTES

Bearing in mind the nature of purchases for which these Shortened Form Conditions will be used, and the limited lead time that will normally apply to the items of equipment covered by them, the Contractor should be in a position to evaluate the risk element involved, and price accordingly.

CLAUSE 15. CONFIDENTIALITY

The Contractor and the Customer shall keep confidential any information obtained under the Contract and shall not divulge the same to any third party without the consent in writing of the other party.

---

*As in the case of the clause in the Main Conditions (Clause 25), the original British clause has been retained as an example. It should be replaced by the normal statutory regulations clause operative in the Customer's locality, perferably in a shortened form on the basis of the above rationale.

Shortened Form of Model Form

EXPLANATORY NOTES

This Shortened Form clause requires both parties to maintain Confidentiality unless consent is given to the other in writing.

CLAUSE 16. MAINTENANCE

If required by the Customer, the Contractor shall enter into a separate Contract for the Maintenance of the Equipment on terms and conditions to be agreed. Maintenance charges during the first year after the acceptance of the Equipment shall reflect the Contractor's obligations under Clause 12.

EXPLANATORY NOTES

When buying computer Equipment of any kind, the question of Maintenance is important and must not be overlooked. The reader is advised to consider this Shortened Form clause in relation to the comments made against the clause in the Main Conditions.

CLAUSE 17. SOFTWARE

Unless otherwise stated in the Contract, the Contractor shall be responsible for providing within the Contract Price all Software and associated documentation necessary for the satisfactory operation of the Equipment.

EXPLANATORY NOTES

Much of the Equipment for which the Shortened Form Conditions will be used will not require separate Software application packages for operational purposes, but the clause does put the obligation on the Contractor to supply any Software and documentation required for the satisfactory operation of the Equipment.

CLAUSE 18. FORCE MAJEURE
Neither party shall be liable for failure to perform its obligations under the Contract if such failure results from circumstances beyond the party's reasonable control.

EXPLANATORY NOTES

Although the intention of this clause is quite clear (neither party should be penalized for failing to carry out his obligations where prevented from doing so by a major force outside his control), care should be exercised in its application.

CLAUSE 19. ATTACHMENTS TO THE EQUIPMENT
The Customer shall have the right to attach to the Equipment free of charge any Equipment not supplied by the Contractor unless the Contractor shall prove to the satisfaction of the Customer that such attachment would be incompatible with and detrimental to the efficient operation of the Equipment.

EXPLANATORY NOTES

The Customer obviously wants to be unrestricted in the use of the Equipment he purchases, but wants to know if Attachments would be incompatible or detrimental to the efficient operation of the Equipment.

The way this clause is written gives the Customer the right to attach other Equipment free of charge, and the only way the Contractor can make a charge is if he proves the Attachment is detrimental. The only time that this situation is likely to arise is where additional costs arise during the Warranty Period or on a Maintenance Contract awarded to the same Contractor.

CLAUSE 20. TRAINING
The Contract Price shall include charges for instruction of the

Customer's personnel in the use of the Equipment and Software, in accordance with the requirements of the Contract.

EXPLANATORY NOTES

This Shortened Form of the main clause on training has the same basic requirement for the Contractor to provide all the necessary training, and here again it is advisable for the extent of training to be established before the Contract is placed. The problems associated with failure to establish the extent of training are, however, unlikely to be very severe, since training requirements for simple Equipment are usually minimal.

CLAUSE 21. PUBLICITY

Neither the Contractor nor his Subcontractors shall, without the prior written consent of the Customer, advertise or publicly announce that he is undertaking work for the Customer.

EXPLANATORY NOTES

This clause is the same as in the Main Conditions.

CLAUSE 22. MANUALS

The Contract Price shall include the provision by the Contractor to the Customer—by not later than the date for delivery of the Equipment—of one set of all documents necessary for the installation, operation, and Maintenance of the Equipment.

EXPLANATORY NOTES

In the case of minor items and peripherals, there is usually no problem in the supply of an Operating Manual with the Equipment purchased, but the Customer should recognize that there may be circumstances where he cannot operate the Equipment satisfactorily until he has the Manual and, in those instances, should withhold payment until the Manual is provided.

CLAUSE 23. TERMINATION

Either party shall have the right to terminate the Contract if the other party is in fundamental breach of the Contract and does not rectify such breach within 14 days of receipt of notification thereof in writing.

EXPLANATORY NOTES

This clause might be a statement of the obvious, but for the time limit involved. In law the fundamental breach of a condition of Contract (as opposed to a breach of warranty) renders the Contract void or voidable at the option of the injured party, who is also entitled to damages arising from the breach.

Establishing this situation in law is not, however, always practical in relation to the time scales applicable to the supply of the type of Equipment intended to be covered by these Shortened Form Conditions. Once again, bearing in mind the alternatives likely to be available to the user, he will want to be free to pursue his requirements, without compromising his position in law, and to be free to obtain the Equipment from another source.

CLAUSE 24. LAW*

Unless otherwise agreed in writing, the Contract shall be construed and interpreted in accordance with the laws of England.

*As in the "how" clause in the Main Conditions (Clause 38), the original clause is retained and the above note is entirely relevant.

EXPLANATORY NOTES

Again, as in the Main Conditions, if the Contract is to be construed in accordance with laws other than those of England, then the country in question should be named.

Postscript

This postscript is intended to draw together some of the threads that run through the whole book.

One theme that is constantly either stated or implied is that a reasonable commercial attitude should be adopted on all contractual issues, and the comments have all been written on that basis. This could evoke criticism from the lawyers, who can say with justification that the comments about the various clauses do not cover all the legal nuances. This is true, since the book is based on practical experience of computer procurement and is designed as a practical aid to the person who is buying computer equipment and wants some basic protection. The clauses in the Model Conditions of Contract should ensure that complicated legal issues do not arise, but in the event of a dispute that cannot be settled amicably between the parties on the basis of the Conditions, legal advice should be sought.

Such disputes should not, however, arise out of any legal deficiencies in the Conditions themselves, because they have been referred to legal advisers at the various stages of production, and were subject to a final examination by the Legal Subcommittee of the IPS Technical Advisory Committee. Where advice of a legal nature is given in the book, it is based on the information given by legal advisers over the period of the working parties' activities in response to general or specific questions, and is my own understanding of the position. However, much law is set by precedent and is constantly developing. I can only repeat that if legal disputes arise, it is best to get professional advice.

Disputes are far more likely to arise out of many manufacturers' Conditions of Sale where, because of the omissions, expensive and complicated legal wrangles could occur when a Contractor disclaims liability and such liabilities have to be established by litigation.

The attitude of some DP managers is just the opposite from that of the lawyers: They consider the whole thing too complicated, and take the view that they have never had any contractual difficulties on Contracts that were based on the manufacturers' Conditions of Sale, so why change? As previously stated, it is only when disputes arise that the Customer wishes he had had protective clauses in his Contract. With no protective clauses, the Customer can still avoid disputes by paying what the Contractor asks, but if that means paying more than would otherwise be necessary, then clearly an unsatisfactory commercial situation exists.

In practice it is no more difficult to issue a request for proposals on the basis of Model Conditions of Contract than to leave it to the manufacturer to specify his own conditions. Furthermore, the receipt of bids on a uniform commercial basis has considerable advantages during the evaluation of offers.

But whether bids are received on the basis of Model Conditions of Contract or of the manufacturers' Conditions of Sale, it is for the Customer to consider whether, in the light of his own essential requirements, there are any specific clauses which he must insist be included in the Contract. This book sets out those individual clauses and the reasons for their normal inclusion. No longer need the Customer start from a blank sheet of paper or try to adapt unsatisfactory standard purchase conditions when faced with the usual omissions from manufacturers' Conditions of Sale.

It is my hope that the value of Model Conditions of Contract will be recognized by computer users and that manufacturers will quickly accept them. Meanwhile it is for each Customer to ensure that the protection afforded by the clauses in the Model Conditions of Contract be embodied in his invitations to bid and to insist on quotations on that basis. Even the largest manufacturers will have to acquiesce if enough Customers demand the inclusion of such provisions in Contracts.